BIZARRE BLUEGRASS

STRANGE BUT TRUE KENTUCKY TALES

KEVEN McQUEEN

ILLUSTRATIONS BY LUCY ELLIOTT

THE
History
PRESS

Published by The History Press
Charleston, SC
www.historypress.com

First published 2020

Manufactured in the United States

ISBN 9781467146784

Library of Congress Control Number: 2020938786

Notice: The information in this book is true and complete to the best of our knowledge. It is offered without guarantee on the part of the author or The History Press. The author and The History Press disclaim all liability in connection with the use of this book.

CONTENTS

Acknowledgements   5

Little-Known Lincoln Stories   7
Kentucky Ghost Towns   21
Two Missing Persons   28
Don't Give Up the Day Job   48
Blue Goon of Kentucky   53
Some Mother's Boy   59
Pearl's Head   62
Circus Trouble   67
Don't Get Back to Where You Once Belonged, Jo-Jo   75
Clay County Creepiness   79
The Great Madison County Monkey Hoax   85
Charivari Shakedowns   93
Professor Tobin Baffles Louisville, Then the World   100
The Second Beethoven's First   107
Charles Manson Surprises an Idiot   110

Bibliography   117
About the Author   128

ACKNOWLEDGEMENTS

The beleaguered author would like to thank:

Eastern Kentucky University Department of English and Theatre; Eastern Kentucky University Interlibrary Loan Department; Amy McQueen and Quentin Hawkins; Daniel Allen Hearn; Jeffrey, Denise and Amber Hughes; Darrell and Swecia McQueen; Darren, Alison and Elizabeth McQueen; Kyle McQueen; Michael, Lori and Blaine McQueen and Evan Holbrook; Chad Rhoad, Ryan Finn and everyone at Arcadia Publishing/The History Press; Craig and Debbie Smith; and Mia Temple. Also: The Ineffable.

LITTLE-KNOWN LINCOLN STORIES

Crumbling old newspapers contain forgotten accounts of even the best-known historical figures, including Abraham Lincoln, one of the most thoroughly written-about men who ever lived. These stories appear in roughly chronological order, beginning before Lincoln's birth and ending after his death.

THE MARRIAGE OF LINCOLN'S PARENTS

Judge J.P. Mitchell lived on a farm seven miles west of Danville, where he built the first two-story house in Boyle County. One of his frequent guests was Nancy Hanks, and one of her frequent guests was Thomas Lincoln. Legend holds that the couple decided to get married while visiting Mitchell's house. Lincoln borrowed one of Judge Mitchell's horses and rode with Nancy to Washington County, where Reverend Jesse Head performed the ceremony on June 12, 1806. Tradition holds also that the couple honeymooned at Mitchell's home. It would be wonderful if this historically significant house still existed, but it burned down in January 1901.

Many decades after the wedding, Reverend Head's grandson was Harrodsburg's postmaster during the Civil War. A rival who wanted the job attempted to get him fired, and Head was sufficiently alarmed that he traveled to Washington to make his case before Lincoln himself. The president was most interested when he discovered the name of his petitioner, stating, "Mr. Head, you say you are located at Harrodsburg, Kentucky?"

"Yes, sir."

"How far is that place from Beechland, in Washington County?"

Fortunately, Head knew his geography. He replied, "Harrodsburg is the county seat of Mercer, which joins Washington County on the east, and Beechland is some twenty-one or two miles from where I live."

"Are you related to or a descendant of a Methodist preacher named Jesse Head, or do you know anything of such a man?"

"He was my grandfather, sir."

Lincoln got up and left the room for a few minutes. He returned with his family Bible. He opened it to show Mr. Head the record proving that his grandfather had united Lincoln's parents.

"Rest assured I shall not forget you at the proper time," said Lincoln. He proved as good as his word.

A NEIGHBOR'S MEMORIES

Eighty-five-year-old Richard Jones had interesting stories to tell a visiting *Louisville Courier-Journal* reporter in October 1902, for Jones was one of the few surviving people who remembered Lincoln's boyhood near Dale, Spencer County, Indiana. Jones showed the journalist a four-acre orchard that John Jones, his father, had hired Lincoln to clear during three months around the spring of 1827, paying young Abraham for his work with bacon and corn. "He was not talkative," recalled Jones, "and seemed particularly taciturn on affairs that related to his home, his father and stepmother....It may have been on the four acres you see over there that Lincoln gained his first experience in splitting rails. Much of the timber was unfit for use, but what there was he turned into rails, and some of these were still preserved in fences on the farm when Lincoln became president."

Later, the Lincolns moved to Illinois, but Jones saw Abraham when he made brief visits to Indiana. On one memorable occasion during an election, which Jones remembered was held on August 1, 1844, a group of men gathered to vote at a schoolhouse. A slouch-hatted Lincoln rode up on horseback, dismounted and greeted every man present by name, although he had not seen some of them in a dozen years or more. The men cried out for a speech from the rising politician, which Lincoln reluctantly delivered. "It was all extemporaneous," remembered Jones, "but the effect was magical. He spoke for an hour, and he held the breathless attention of every man. Then, with a 'Well, boys, I must go now,' he rode away as suddenly as he came, and he never visited southern Indiana again."

Jones finished his reminiscences: "In those days we little dreamed of the importance to which this ungainly man would arise later in life. We knew him as just plain 'Abe' Lincoln. We had a sincere respect for him. He was a man that could always command respect. He was 'Honest Abe.'"

PROVING A POINT

In 1906, a Republican leader in Philadelphia related one of lawyer Lincoln's cleverest legal stratagems. A rival attorney had argued that a certain will was genuine; Lincoln's task was to prove that it wasn't. The rival spent hours providing evidence in the will's favor. To courtroom observers, it seemed that Lincoln was fighting a lost cause—particularly when he put only one witness on the stand. What followed must have been one of the briefest routs in the history of American law. Lincoln handed the disputed will to his witness—who happened to be a retired paper manufacturer—and said, "Please hold that paper up to the light and tell us what is the watermark on it."

"The watermark of my own firm."

"When did your firm begin to manufacture paper?"

"In 1841."

"And what's the date on the document in your hands?"

"August 11, 1836."

"That is enough. Gentlemen of the jury, our case is closed."

THE LINCOLN-SHIELDS DUEL

One of the most obscure events in Lincoln's life is a duel that he nearly fought in 1842 with James Shields, then the state auditor of Illinois and later a distinguished general in the Civil War. The trouble began when an anonymous author known only as "Aunt Rebecca" wrote a series of letters to the *Sangamo Journal* (the *Springfield Journal* in some accounts) ridiculing Shields for everything ranging from his Irish ancestry to his alleged lack of courage to his dandified ways. According to the writer, Shields went "floatin' about the air, without heft or earthly substance, just like a lock of cat-fur where cats had been fighting." Infuriated, Shields vowed to fight a duel if he found out the author's identity. This inspired "Aunt Rebecca" to offer to let Shields "squeeze her hand":

> *If this should not answer, there is one thing more I would do rather than get a lickin'. I have all along expected to die a widow; but, as Mr. S. is rather good looking than otherwise, I must say I don't care if we compromise the matter by—really, Mr. Printer, I can't help blushin'—but I—it must come out—but widowed modesty—well, if I must I must—wouldn't he—maybe sorter, let the old grudge drap* [sic] *if I was to consent to be—be—h-i-s w-i-f-e!*

And much more in this vein. Shields became convinced that Lincoln was the writer; he may have been right, although many believed the actual culprit was Lincoln's fiancée, Mary Todd. In any case, Lincoln refused to admit or deny authorship, and on September 22, he and Shields crossed the river into Missouri to fight with broad swords (dueling had been illegal in Illinois since 1839). The story goes that Shields changed his mind when he realized that the extraordinarily tall Lincoln could reach farther with a sword than he. Shields called off the fight—probably to Lincoln's secret relief—and the two became friends. Lincoln married Mary Todd two months later. Later in life, he seemed embarrassed whenever the topic of his duel came up.

Even less understood than the affray with Shields is the fact that Lincoln may have barely avoided fighting *another* duel two years before. In January 1899, historian J. Stoddard Johnston told of letters he had found in the library of the Tennessee Historical Society at Nashville. The first, written by W.G. Anderson of Lawrenceville, Illinois, on October 30, 1840, was addressed to Lincoln; as Johnston noted, beneath Anderson's studiedly polite language he seemed to be spoiling for a fight:

> *On our first meeting on Wednesday last a difficulty in words ensued between us, which I deem it my duty to notice further. I think you were the aggressor. Your words imported an insult; and whether you meant them as such is for you to say. You will, therefore, please inform me on this point, and if you designed to offend me, please communicate to me your present feelings on the subject, and whether you persist in the stand you took.*

Lincoln replied the next day:

> *Your note of yesterday is received. In the difficulty between us of which you speak, you say you think I was the aggressor. I do not think I was. You say my "words imported insult." I meant them as a fair set-off to your own statements, and not otherwise; and in that light alone I now wish you to understand them. You ask for my "present feelings on the subject." I entertain no unkind feeling to you, except a sincere regret that I permitted myself to get into such an altercation.*

There, it appears, the matter rested.

SUPERIOR SOCKS, BATTERED HAT

Lincoln emancipated the slaves and kept the union together. He also knew good socks when he saw them. In 1861, Susannah Weathers of Rossville, Clinton County, Indiana, sent the new president a letter and a pair of handmade socks. Lincoln took time from his harrowing war schedule to send her this seldom-reprinted reply:

> *Executive Mansion, Washington, Dec. 4, 1861.—My Dear Madam: I take great pleasure in acknowledging the receipt of your letter of November 26, and in thanking you for the present by which it was accompanied—a pair of socks so fine and soft and warm could hardly have been manufactured in any other way than the old Kentucky fashion. Your letter informs me that your maiden name was Crume, and that you were raised in Washington County, Ky., by which I infer that an uncle of mine by marriage was a relative of yours. Nearly, or quite, sixty years ago, Ralph Crume married Mary Lincoln, a sister of my father, in Washington County, Ky. Accept my thanks and believe me very truly your friend, A. LINCOLN.*

Lincoln's most famous item of clothing was, of course, his stovepipe hat, which he often used for storing letters and important documents. In 1896, many years after his death, an unnamed Springfield resident told writer Francis Leon Chrisman of a joyous, if undignified, use for Lincoln's hat on the night in 1860 when he and his neighbors learned by telegram that he had won the presidency. "A few of us ladies went over and helped Mrs.

Lincoln prepare a little supper for her friends who had been invited in to hear the returns," she recalled. When the good news finally came, Lincoln's neighbors spontaneously took his hat off a rack and commenced playing an indoors game of football with it—ladies included.

MOSBY'S TAUNT

During the Civil War, Colonel John S. Mosby was the leader of Mosby's Rangers, one of the most feared bands of Confederate guerrillas. In one of those surreal moments that make history so much fun, in August 1911, nearly a half century after the war ended, Mosby once again put on his old uniform and strapped on his sword to re-create his raids for a motion picture company. As the movie technicians set up their cameras and equipment on location just outside Washington, D.C., Mosby served as what we today would call a technical advisor. He also regaled reporters, actors and bystanders with stories about the war, including the following amusing incident.

In 1861, as Mosby rode along the Virginia side of the Potomac, he saw an elderly woman peddling vegetables. Then he thought of a way to taunt the Union's chief executive. Borrowing a pair of scissors from the peddler, Mosby cut off a lock of his hair and handed it to her with these instructions: "Take this to President Lincoln in the White House and tell him that Mosby will be over in a few days to take a similar keepsake from his head."

Mosby rode on and forgot about his joke. A few months later, he revisited the area. The old vegetable peddler saw him and ran out of her cabin brandishing an envelope. "Col. Mosby," said she, "President Lincoln told me to give you this and tell you he would rather send it to you than put you to the trouble of coming over after it." The envelope contained a lock of Lincoln's hair.

"I MADE YOU PRESIDENT"

Lincoln was plagued with office seekers throughout his presidency. Frederic J. Haskin told an anecdote about a markedly obnoxious and persistent one who claimed that Lincoln owed him a job since he was personally responsible for making Lincoln president.

"You made me president, did you?" asked Lincoln.

"I am sure I did."

"Well, if you really did, you ought to be ashamed of yourself for the mess you got me into."

WHITE HOUSE WEDDING

In August 1861, James Henry Chandler of Bowling Green, Kentucky, had a heart-wrenching problem. He had moved to Augusta County, Virginia, where he fell in love with a sixteen-year-old girl named Elizabeth Sheets. Her parents objected to the match because she was too young. Therefore, Henry and Elizabeth eloped to nearby Washington, D.C. They found themselves bewildered by their surroundings, having never been in such a large city before, and realized that they had not arranged in advance for a location at which to tie the knot. Out of sheer naïveté, they went to the White House to see if anyone objected to their getting married there. As she later explained, they thought "it'd be sorta fine like to have a White House wedding, and we didn't think Mr. Lincoln'd mind much if we borrowed his house, as it was too big for him to use all of it, anyway." She remembered that she wore a blue cashmere dress, and her groom wore a shiny alpaca suit.

One interesting subtext to the Chandlers' story is that it tells us something about the lax security measures in those days. Despite the fact that the Civil War was raging and Confederates in nearby Virginia were thirsting to invade Washington, Henry and Elizabeth appear to have walked unchallenged right up to the White House doors. A porter let them into the house, and within moments the president himself greeted them. As Mrs. Chandler remembered, "I don't remember so much about Mr. Lincoln, except that I wished Henry's coat was long like his. But I remember thinking Henry was a lot handsomer."

The president smiled and said, "So you children want to be married? Come right in and we'll get at the marrying." Lincoln sent for a Baptist minister. The bride later recalled, "Pretty soon the minister came and Mr. Lincoln rang some kind of a bell and it seems as if a hundred people came running in—the ladies all dressed so fine that my blue cashmere just didn't seem pretty at all. The men were grand, too, but Henry looked as good as any of them. Henry knew how to act; he'd been in big houses before."

Henry and Elizabeth were married in a room that impressed her as being "the biggest room, all draped with flags" and having a shiny floor. Lincoln then insisted the couple have a bite to eat and complimented the self-conscious country girl on her dress:

> *I guess he went out to tell Mrs. Lincoln to have it pipin' hot on the table. I can't rightly remember Mrs. Lincoln, but I think she must have been the woman that came up to him while we were waiting for the parson and said, "Abe, what foolishness are you up to now with your office full of people?" He didn't say anything—just went on about the marryin' and talkin' nice to Henry and me, and telling me how glad he was my dress was blue, because he always liked blue cashmere.*

Aides led the newlyweds to "a big dining-room." More than sixty years after the event, Elizabeth related, "I never ate so much food in all my life—such eating! Things I never heard tell of, all set on the biggest table in the biggest room I ever saw!" Apparently, the guests at the impromptu wedding reception made toasts: "I remember they served something to drink that they called hot punch, and now and then all would stand while someone said something and then all would drink hot punch." Afterward there was a dance, but for Lincoln the undoubtedly welcome distraction was over. He returned to his office to get back to work. "As he left he said 'God bless you children and thank you for coming to the White House for your marryin'.'"

The couple asked some attendants what they would be charged for the wedding and the food, only to be told that it was free. The president had invited them to stay overnight at the White House, "and we did stay. The next day we went back up the Potomac and crossed at Harper's Ferry and then got back to our homes, where they forgave us and were surprised that we got married in the White House."

Soon after their marriage, James Henry Chandler joined the Union army and fought until the end of the war. The Chandlers moved to Anderson, Indiana, where they lived the rest of their lives. Elizabeth told the story to a reporter in February 1906, when she was an elderly widow, and again February 1929.

Lincoln's Substitute

During the Civil War, a well-to-do man could hire someone else to enlist in the army and fight in his place. It is a little-known fact of history that Lincoln himself had a substitute in battle. As chief executive, Lincoln was exempt from the draft, but felt he should have some personal representative on the field of war to set an example for the nation. Thus, in 1864, he hired nineteen-year-old Private John Summerfield Staples of Stroudsburg, Pennsylvania. Government records show that Staples had formerly served in Company C of the 176th Pennsylvania Militia from November 2, 1862, until his honorable discharge on May 5, 1863. As Lincoln's substitute, Staples enlisted in Company H of the Second District of Columbia Volunteers on April 3, 1864. He served with distinction until he got his second honorable discharge on September 12, 1865.

Staples died on January 11, 1888, at age forty-three. In 1910, there was talk of building a $20,000 monument to Staples's memory.

HIS OLD FRIEND ABE LINCOLN

Nearly fifty years after the end of the war, the widow of Confederate general George Pickett told a story that well illustrates Lincoln's humility. In 1865, after Federal troops had seized Richmond, Virginia, Lincoln toured the captured city, which happened to be where the Picketts lived. As the president explored the town, he saw the general's house. He knocked on the door, and when Mrs. Pickett answered, Lincoln asked, "Does George Pickett live here?"

He received an icy response. "*General* Pickett lives here, sir, but he is not at home; he is with the army under General Lee."

Lincoln mildly replied, "Well, will you please tell him when he returns that his old friend Abe Lincoln called to see him? I wish you good day, madam." Then he walked away.

When recounting the story, Mrs. Pickett commented, "From that day, I have always had the greatest respect for Mr. Lincoln." Significantly, her surprise caller didn't identify himself as *President* Lincoln, but as Abe Lincoln—an old friend. Long before, Pickett had been a cadet at West Point and was on the verge of expulsion for some infraction. While Pickett's trial was impending, he went on furlough. He visited relatives who lived near Springfield, Illinois, and who happened to know an up-and-coming attorney named Lincoln. They hired him, and he successfully petitioned West Point to keep Pickett as a cadet. Pickett graduated with honor just as the Mexican-American War began; he served in that war with distinction and went to become a top-ranking Confederate general. The deep irony is that Lincoln had saved the military career of a man who, decades later, would fight for the Confederacy.

THE BED AT THE PETERSEN HOUSE

Lloyd Moxley, long ago the city bill-poster of Washington, D.C., told a bizarre story about the president's assassination to the *Washington Post* in November 1895. Readers are advised to treat it with caution. According to Moxley, he had been a theatrical manager and thus had a passing acquaintance with John Wilkes Booth. On the night of April 14, 1865, Moxley had been standing outside the president's box at Ford's Theater when Booth showed up. The two chatted for several minutes, and then Moxley left and Booth completed his mission.

Bystanders carried the wounded Lincoln to the Petersen boardinghouse across the street. Moxley, noting that the house often tenanted actors, claimed that Booth had rented a room there the week of the assassination—and that Lincoln died in the same bed on which his killer had tried to take a nap earlier in the day. While it is possible that Lincoln died in a bed that Booth had rented at some time in the past, William T. Clark was renting the room on the fatal night.

DESTRUCTION OF BOOTH'S PROPERTY

Collectors of Americana have noted that few personal items belonging to John Wilkes Booth are still in existence. The reason is that the assassin's brother, actor Edwin Booth, waged a one-man campaign to make sure there was nothing left. Three years after Edwin's death, Garrison Davidson, Booth's theatrical property man, related that the actor had feared that any items of his brother's "might be hawked about the country, pandering to the depraved curiosity of vulgar people." The government sent trunks full of John's clothes to Edwin's theater in New York. One morning, Edwin enlisted Davidson's help for a mysterious chore, which turned out to be the destruction in the theater's basement furnace of every item of memorabilia from the trunks. Davidson said that it broke his heart (and Edwin's) to throw such fine clothing into the fire, and he asked the tragedian if he might keep a particularly luxurious fur coat.

"No, Garry," said Booth, "It must not be. There is no man living I would more willingly give that coat to than you. But I cannot endure the thought that any man, not even you, Garry, is wearing a coat that my poor, misguided brother had worn. It must disappear in the flames forever." In addition to clothes, Edwin tossed into the fire—after much hesitation and many tears—a jeweled dagger given to the Booth brothers' father, Junius Brutus, by the British actor William Macready. Edwin smashed the emptied trunks with an axe and threw the pieces into the furnace.

A side note: Perhaps due its scarcity, as of 1879 Booth's autograph was worth more than his victim's. At an auction held in Boston that year, Lincoln's signature went for $11.25 (which would be the equivalent of slightly over $240 in modern currency), while Booth's sold for $25 (about $500). By 1905, however, Lincoln's autograph was selling for $100 at a Chicago auction (modern equivalent: slightly over $2,400), which made it more valuable than George Washington's, a signature by whom sold at the same auction for $28 ($680).

LINCOLN'S ABANDONED LUXURY CAR

In 1864, the United States military hired B.P. Lamason to build a special private railroad car for the president at Alexandria, Virginia. The car was forty-two feet long by eight and a half feet wide and divided into three compartments: two small rooms and a large one used as an office and study for consulting with civilian, governmental and military guests. Crimson silk covered the walls, and the large room included frieze work decorated with painted renditions of various state seals. The rooms were "handsomely furnished" with such comforts as framed pictures, sofas and upholstered reclining chairs. An extra-long sofa accommodated the lanky president, and it could be converted into a sort of bunk bed consisting of an upper and lower berth. The outside platform of the car had brass railings, and the car itself was clad in armor inside and out, making it bulletproof. (Think of it as the nineteenth-century equivalent of *Air Force One*.) It weighed so much that it was mounted on four four-wheeled trucks. Lincoln used the finished product to visit New York and Philadelphia and the Army of the Potomac in Virginia. When Lincoln died, the car became part of his funeral train.

After the war, the government auctioned the car (and other unused railway material) in Cincinnati, where T.C. Durant purchased it in 1866 on behalf of the Union Pacific Railroad. The company intended to use it as a private car for its directors, but it was too heavy and cumbersome for practical use. At some point, Sidney Dillon, a Union Pacific executive, had the furniture removed and sent to New York. After Durant and Dillon passed away, Lincoln's pride and joy was employed as a dining car for a railroad construction gang out west. Then it was brought to the Union Pacific yard in Omaha, and there, for unknown reasons, it was simply deserted.

Late in 1892, a company of New Yorkers opened negotiations to purchase the decrepit car with the intention of making it a world's fair exhibit. No one could agree on a price, and the scheme, like the car itself, was ignominiously abandoned. In 1897, the *Chicago Tribune* described the rotting relic: "Its sides are cracked and weather-beaten, and the glass in its windows and the brass railings on its platforms are long ago gone. All the compartments and sumptuous interior furnishings and decorations have been removed, and it stands like a barren, decaying hulk of its own proud self."

Lincoln's car remained forsaken until August 4, 1903, when the Union Pacific sold it to private parties, who displayed it at the St. Louis Exposition.

LINCOLN RELICS

W.D. Woffall owned a truly remarkable piece of history, having been in the right place at the right time. He attended the play *Our American Cousin* on the night of April 14, 1865, and happened to have the seat below Lincoln's box. Before the play commenced, the audience cheered the president, who stood up to acknowledge their greeting. As he did so, his playbill fell from his hand and fluttered on down to Woffall, who wanted to keep it as a souvenir of a memorable occasion. He had no idea just how memorable that occasion was going to be, but then John Wilkes Booth made his unasked-for onstage appearance. As of 1903, Woffall had given the program to his friend A.F. Hawthorn, a manufacturer from Lancaster, Pennsylvania.

Dr. M.B. Emery of Carlisle, Nicholas County, Kentucky, formerly of Springfield, Illinois, owned an axe given to him by Lincoln, who had used it to split rails. In 1903, the doctor said he had refused offers of up to $5,000 for the axe.

W.W. Glass, a farmer of Maryville, Missouri, was the proud owner of a dictionary that had belonged to Thomas Lincoln and was passed down to Abraham. The book, found in the attic of a Hancock County, Kentucky log cabin, had the charming title *An Universal Etymological English Dictionary and Interpreter of Hard Words*. Curiously, the book had an unexplained bullet hole in the cover. In October 1912, Glass gave the dictionary to the State Historical Society of Missouri.

Lincoln made a walnut cabinet, which eventually passed to U.S. commissioner J.W. Wartmann of Evansville, Indiana. A newspaper article reported that when Wartmann's house caught fire in December 1907, he "directed the firemen to save the cabinet if they had to let everything else

burn." Fortunately, the cabinet was saved with one corner burned off and some damage done to correspondence between Wartmann and Lincoln's old law partner William Herndon.

A sad story hit the nation's press in November 1904, when a ninety-year-old former slave, Alexander Freeman, sued a New York City express company for $300 for losing an overcoat that had belonged to Lincoln, who had given it to Freeman in 1864, when he worked as a servant in the White House.

One of the best stories about relics Lincoln left behind concerns a cane and gavel, both made of black walnut and presented in 1860 to his friend Ira Haworth, chairman of the Township Committee in Springfield, Illinois. Lincoln whittled the cane himself. Haworth remembered that Lincoln presented the gifts with these words: "The gavel is to keep order. The cane is to use when you get old. I know you will live to be old, because the good die young."

KENTUCKY GHOST TOWNS

We associate ghost towns with the Wild West, but every region of America has them. Kentucky has several, and the stories behind them are varied and interesting. Residents abandoned some towns, while others never really existed.

GRANARD, FAYETTE COUNTY. In 1885, several prominent men—notably wealthy Irish grocer Dennis Mulligan and Judge James Mulligan—chartered fifty-two acres adjacent to Lexington's northern limits. They named the area Granard and then failed to do anything with it. Although legally considered a town, Granard never had streets, city officials, a fire department, a police force or anything else. The landowners incorporated the property to prevent the Belt Line railroad from constructing tracks on it, but after the railroad was built close to the property anyway, they did nothing more to develop it. As of 1897, the sole inhabitant was a German dairyman, Fred Haldeman, who dwelled in Granard's only house. There was talk of building a pool hall on the property after Lexington forbade the construction of the same within city limits, but nothing seems to have come of the scheme. In March 1914, it was announced that "the mythical town," which was estimated to be worth $300,000, would at last be sold. Granard is a town that existed almost entirely on paper, but there is still a street in Lexington bearing the proud name Granard Avenue.

MARTINSVILLE, WARREN COUNTY. Founded in 1820 by Dr. Hudson Martin, Martinsville was located ten and a half miles east of Bowling Green. For a few decades, it was a thriving river town complete with a store, a warehouse, a distillery, and flatboats that freighted tobacco to New Orleans. By the 1840s, Martinsville was at its peak and averaging one good fistfight every day. But grand steamboats and the L&N Railroad put humble flatboats out of business, and a rumor that the local spring water was unhealthy scared off inhabitants. All that remained to commemorate the once-booming city was an area of the Barren River known as the Martinsville ford. In 1902, a newspaper reporter eulogized the town: "Not a token or a trace remains, for the graveyard is far away and completely overgrown with a forest of large trees. But the tombstones tell the sad story of the town—fine monuments, modest slabs and unpretending mementoes tell the tragedy alike of those who sleep beneath and of the once proud city of Martinsville."

FLORENCE STATION, MCCRACKEN COUNTY. The town was one of the oldest stations on the Illinois Central Railroad line until business moved elsewhere. In July 1905, the community ceased to be a stop on the route and was soon "off the map." As railroad employees dismantled the depot, they flew a flag bearing the sad inscription "Goodbye, Florence, goodbye."

LYSTRA, NELSON COUNTY. The third volume of Colonel Winterbotham's book *Historical, Geological, Commercial, and Philosophical View of the American United States* (London, 1795) refers to "the promising city of Lystra, in

Nelson County, Ky.," fifteen thousand acres in size and located on the south side of the Rolling Fork River, between Salt Lick and Otter Creek. The book included a map of the town, a neatly laid-out community of twenty-five blocks with one-hundred-foot-wide parallel thoroughfares bearing names such as Orchard Street, Vine Street, Jefferson and Nelson. Sites for churches, a college, markets, a town hall and theaters were in the center of town. There was also a "common meadow" where all inhabitants could graze their horses.

Perhaps the reader is darkly muttering, "Why, I've never heard of this major Kentucky metropolis!" With good cause: Lystra does not exist—and never did. It was a hoax dreamed up by the British publishers of the book allegedly written by Colonel Winterbotham. "Hoax" is actually too kind a word; it was a *scam* designed to lure Britons to purchase unsold lots in the fictitious city. The volume included an advertisement: "Lots undisposed of may be purchased at the Agency Office, Threadneedle Street, London." Some enthusiastic dupes not only bought stock in the Lystra Town Company but also even immigrated to Kentucky. Those who took a risky ocean voyage to check out the site in person were due for a rude disappointment. Lystra was as nonexistent as Brigadoon. Salt Creek—depicted in Winterbotham's book as large enough to accommodate ships—was but a paltry stream.

The Threadneedle Street swindlers successfully convinced another set of speculators to invest in imaginary Ohio-Piomingo, a convincingly mapped and advertised town allegedly located thirty miles from Louisville.

BEALLSBOROUGH, NELSON COUNTY. Walter Beall, wealthy citizen of Bardstown, was determined to build one of the world's most beautiful cities in Nelson County. In 1796, he bought a tract of land on the south side of the Rolling Fork at the mouth of Beech Fork. Like the con artists who sold Lystra, Beall created a detailed map of his planned utopia, tentatively to be named Beallsborough, but unlike them, he was perfectly sincere in his plan to construct the garden spot of Kentucky. Beall dreamed big ambitious dreams of tobacco warehouses, public buildings and stone chimneys, but he could encourage few to risk their money on his proposed city—after all, Lystra was supposedly a neighboring community, and that was enough to give wary investors second thoughts. Beallsborough was fated never to be.

MORTONSVILLE, WOODFORD COUNTY. While technically not a ghost town—though tiny, Mortonsville still exists—the city never quite lived up to its early promise. Founded in 1790, it was once such a prominent settlement that it missed becoming Kentucky's state capital by only one vote. When trains supplanted trade and travel on the river, Mortonsville declined. Nearby Versailles became the county's premier city.

MILFORD, MADISON COUNTY. In 1786, Kentucky was still part of Virginia, and Governor Patrick Henry of that state appointed a committee to organize a government for the recently formed Madison County. Milford was selected county seat by vote, and pioneers built a log courthouse there (later replaced with a $400 one made of stone). Further additions included a jail, a store, a tannery, a hatmaker, blacksmiths, a number of taverns and a whipping post. By 1787, Milford was home to eighteen families. Kentucky became a state in 1792, and in early 1798, the legislature suggested replacing Milford with Richmond as Madison's county seat. "Over our dead bodies," said the Milfordites as one. The matter was settled pioneer-style in March with a knock-down, drag-out fight between two rowdies: Dave Kennedy, who represented Milford, and William Kearley of Richmond. The honor of being county seat would go to the victor's town. Kennedy and Kearley stripped to the waist, had their heads shaved and were coated with grease to make things more challenging. The "rassling match" degenerated into a frenzy of kicking, punching and ear chawing.

At last, Kearley was declared the winner, and Richmond became the chief settlement of Madison County. The battle wasn't even necessary: by the time it occurred, the legislature in Frankfort had already voted in favor of Richmond, and a delegation had removed the records from the Milford courthouse and transported them to the new county seat—the news had not traveled quickly enough to prevent the brawl. The legislature prevented further violence when it agreed to compensate Milford residents for their lost property values. As of 1939, the courthouse chimney was all that remained of Milford, a town men once thought worth fighting over.

AIRDRIE, MUHLENBERG COUNTY. Once a city on a bluff overlooking Green River, Airdrie was founded in 1855. Sir Robert S.C.A. Alexander planned it as a socialist paradise on earth for his iron furnace workers, yet another in a line of seemingly a half-billion such unsuccessful places that have been planned throughout history. But the hills ran out of ore, and the furnace closed in 1859; that spelled the end for Airdrie.

The spooky ruins of the city remained for decades, and some are visible still. In February 1911, a *Louisville Courier-Journal* reporter described the tumbled-down houses and the streets overgrown with bushes, grass, even the occasional tree. Large stone steps led from the riverbank to the top of the bluff. There was a decrepit iron smelter, and decaying mine cars sat on rusting rails where laborers abandoned them a half century earlier. One recently burned mansion was once home to a celebrity: Union Civil War general Don Carlos Buell.

In Airdrie's prime, law officers forced prisoners to work in the mines. A large uninhabited building was once a prison. (Decades later, John Prine referred to the "abandoned old prison down by Airdrie Hill" in his song "Paradise.") Nearby was an entrance to a massive cave where, it was said, two escaped prisoners hid and never came out. Presumably, their remains are still there.

Rumor held that the ghost town was home to a *real* ghost, a murder victim that haunted the crumbling hotel. "The truth of this story is well established," said a reporter in 1911, while admitting that there were conflicting details. Reportedly, murderers strangled and decapitated a wealthy young woman in a room on the second floor. The killers left her head burning in a fireplace. They took not only her jewelry but also the rest of her body, which was never found. (According to some, her attackers "subjected [her] to every sort of indignity," but how could anyone know that if the body were missing?) The *Courier-Journal* reporter entered the ruin and climbed a rickety staircase to the second floor, where one room had a charred floor—allegedly scorch marks made when the poor woman's smoldering head rolled out of the fireplace. The journalist noted that all of the hotel's furniture had long since been removed except a rotting card table.

MORTALLES, HENDERSON COUNTY. A big announcement came in April 1911. New Yorker J.A. Brown intended to build a model socialist utopian city on an uninviting, mosquito-infested marsh called Horseshoe Bend in Henderson County, on the bank of the Ohio River across from Evansville, Indiana. Brown described the future city as such model places are usually described: there would be "peace and plenty" and "a brotherhood charter" for "a community of brothers." It would launch "an era of a new day," and the city government would run the town competently with "no mayor and no aldermen, no politics and no police, no statutes and no conventions, no competition, no trusts, and no graft"—exactly the kind of place "sordid materialists" had long considered merely "an idle dream." (Spoiler alert: see Airdrie, earlier.)

The ninety-acre city, to be known as Mortalles, already had a powerhouse for supplying electricity and an imposing sixty-foot-tall administration building that housed a café, a ballroom, a billiard hall and a room where gentlemen could play cards. Each room in the building was painted a different lurid color, and the place was outfitted with office equipment and (for reasons unexplained) cash registers. Mortalles also contained a few tents occupied by persons who just couldn't wait to move into the city once the expected flood of world-weary pilgrims arrived and constructed houses.

Mr. Brown enthusiastically told reporters how the city—*not* private businesses!—would own the waterworks, the power plant, the telephone system and so on; how every lot in the city would represent a vote for its landowner; how all the houses would have to meet a pre-approved architectural style; how no one would be permitted to sell a lot without the community's consent; and ever so much, much more. His proposed city would also have no black residents or saloons.

Mother Nature gave Brown fair warning when his powerhouse and administration building both collapsed in a windstorm and heavy rain threatened to flood his utopia on the Ohio. Undaunted, he laboriously rebuilt the wrecked buildings and continued with his former schemes for the new city. He also contemplated a few additional ones, including a railroad to Henderson and a summer theater to attract potential settlers.

The locals—whose opinions about Brown's doings ranged from deep suspicion to unrestrained hilarity—generally referred to Mortalles as "Magic City," "Mysterious City" or "Dream City."

Mortalles withered on the vine. After spending $32,000 worth of his own money and that of his investors, Brown ran out of funds. He platted lots, named roads and built a waterworks in addition to the other two buildings, but his few tenants gave up and left in 1913. The abandoned embryonic city was sold at auction on February 12, 1914, to J.W. Bodine, who made the highest bid at a mere $4,481.78. Perhaps Brown recouped his losses by wisely investing that extra seventy-eight cents.

By 1918, Mortalles was still unused. A reporter described the melancholy remains as "a stretch of wild undergrowth broken here and there with magnificent buildings fast going to decay" and ruined asphalt streets. Although J.A. Brown had declared that his perfect city would never be sullied by a saloon, new owner Richard Pennington applied for a license to turn the large and beautiful—though garishly colored—administration building into a drinking establishment. The local chapter of the Woman's Christian Temperance Union objected, and the never-completed Mortalles, Kentucky, dropped out of the news and the mind of humanity forever.

TWO MISSING PERSONS

Few things are more intriguing to lovers of real-life mysteries than stories about missing persons—people who seem to vanish from the face of the earth. Here are two little-known tales from Kentucky's past, the first bordering on absurdity and the second a creepy, never-solved enigma.

BACK WHEN THE UNIVERSITY of Kentucky was Kentucky State University, one of its freshmen was twenty-year-old Willis Eugene Smith, an agriculture student from Hindman, Knott County. The fall 1908 semester had barely started and Smith had been enrolled for only twenty days when he left his boardinghouse on the night of Tuesday, September 22. On the way out, he told his older brother Ernest, a sophomore, that he was going to a meeting on campus. "I'm going to have some fun," he said. Ernest noticed that Willis wore ratty old clothes and left his money, watch and other valuables behind. Later, it was speculated that he expected hazing or some other rough treatment. He did not return that night.

A sober young man devoted to his family, Willis was an unlikely candidate for dissipation, foul play or running away. As the hours turned into days, Ernest's unease ripened into panic, and he asked the police for help. The leading theory was that some of Willis's classmates were holding him captive as a hazing prank. If true, it would have been a heck of a joke since they worried his family and caused him to miss classes.

The students at Kentucky State (let's just call it UK for convenience's sake!) refused to take Smith's disappearance seriously, but the faculty felt otherwise. On September 24, Professor James G. White admonished the assembled students that the prank, if prank it was, had gone far enough and urged them to release Smith immediately. "[T]here is little doubt that he is safe and well and will be released when his captors believe the joke has gone far enough," remarked a reassuring early press account.

After five days passed with no trace of Smith, it was obvious that his absence was not the result of some harebrained hazing ritual. Was he a kidnapping victim? Had he run away on his own? Worst possibility of all, had he been murdered—perhaps by fellow students, intentionally or due to a prank gone wrong?

The faculty held a special meeting on September 29. They spent a few days interviewing students, all of whom swore they had no idea what had happened to Willis. The students who attended the Tuesday night meeting that had been his destination said he never showed up. Ernest Smith offered a reward of $50 to anyone who could reveal the whereabouts of his brother. The modern equivalent of that sum would be nearly $1,000.

Another brother, Professor A.E. Smith, a Hindman public school principal, arrived in Lexington and hired detectives. Yet another sibling, Frampton

Smith of Owensboro, telegraphed that he had not heard from Willis. A negative reply also came from their father, Willis P. Smith, a Presbyterian minister then in Melrose, New Mexico. The family was convinced that the missing young man had met with foul play. Some Lexingtonians still thought that Smith's fellow students abducted him, reasoning that perhaps he had been injured and they didn't want to release him until he was healed. Alternatively, maybe they were *afraid* to set him free, knowing well the wrath they were certain to face from the university now that their little joke had received so much publicity.

There were three leading theories a week after the disappearance: his fellow students were holding Smith in captivity; Smith was a murder victim; or Smith chose to leave campus on his own volition and, for reasons known only to himself, did not want his family to know he had left. But would he run away leaving nearly all his money in his rented room?

Matters took a sinister turn on October 1. A boy related a story to his father, who retold it to a friend, who shared it with another, until seemingly all of Lexington knew it in minutes. The boy claimed that he had overheard a conversation among UK sophomores in which they admitted that, as a hazing stunt, they had gagged Smith, tied him hand and foot and thrown him into a boxcar. The boys had assumed that he would spend an interesting night in the car, and then trainmen would release him the next day. Then the train took off, taking the unwilling stowaway with it. If the story were true, Smith could be *anywhere*. And what if the boxcar were abandoned on a siding far from town? He could starve before discovery!

Those who believed the story pointed out that UK students had become notorious locally for their antisocial stunts. During Halloween 1906, for example, some of these gentle scholars had cut electric wires, leaving part of the campus in darkness. Live wires on the street lay in wait for someone to step on them. The seekers of higher learning had also built bonfires between streetcar tracks. For a capper, they placed a rock on a streetcar track, nearly causing a wreck that certainly would have caused injuries. Instead of scramming afterward, they formed a surly mob around the car. A force of twenty cops ran them off after a pitched battle, during which students fired shots and hurled a rock that injured police captain Ford. When the rioters were chased back to campus, they attacked a sole policeman who had been sent to guard the women's dormitory. They tore off his coat, helmet, badge and pistol and perfected his humiliation by taking a photo of him in this undignified condition. An investigating grand jury had thundered, "So far as we can determine, the system of discipline at the college is absolutely inefficient.…[W]e find that the authorities at the college have absolutely no effective system of discipline and practically no control over the conduct of the student body."

These incidents explain the palpable animosity Lexington police felt for UK students during the Smith investigation. Captain Ford would call the students "some of the worst boys in America" and remark that if he had a choice between sending his son to UK or to reform school he would choose the latter; Captain Jenkins and Sergeant Shea said that the school "is pretty near the most lawless place in the country." Referring to one of the state's most violent and feud-ridden places, they added, "It is infinitely worse than Breathitt County in its palmiest days." The cops were also annoyed when UK's president, James K. Patterson, took up for the students and complained when the police forced the young hellions back on school grounds. Lexington police were convinced that someone had pulled strings to help the rioters escape with light punishment.

People who lived near the tracks said that rowdy college students indeed had been skylarking in the area on the night of Smith's disappearance, and the university confirmed that some students had hazed others at the time and that some of the incidents were violent—in fact, one freshman fired shots through his room door at his tormentors.

A few days after his brother disappeared, Ernest Smith got a letter bearing the print of a black hand with the message, "You had better stop this investigation." The Black Hand consisted almost entirely of Italian hoods who extorted money from Italian merchants, so the idea that there was a chapter of the organization in Lexington with an interest in threatening a college student was laughable (but not laughable to Ernest Smith). Most onlookers considered the anonymous letter a tacky practical joke.

Meanwhile, detectives complained that UK was less than helpful in aiding their investigation. Officers had no authority to examine campus buildings or students' rooms, for example, yet university officials dithered over conducting a search themselves. President Patterson retorted that school officials were now convinced their pupils were innocent: "I do not believe now that the students had anything to do with it. At first, I thought it was possible that young Smith may have been concealed as a joke, but as he has not appeared, I am now confident that the boys of the university know nothing about the case. You see, Mr. Smith had only recently matriculated and was therefore unknown to the great body of the students." He added that the police were welcome to inspect the university's buildings.

On October 1, a committee formed by UK and headed by four professors dropped more than just a broad hint that they thought Smith had engineered his own disappearance: "All the information at hand seems to indicate that he has left the city. Unfortunately, what little information we have cannot be made public, but we hope that the public will withhold criticism at least for the present." Certainly, school and local authorities were taking the mystery seriously. A press account dated October 2 said the incident "stirred up this city, the university, and the surrounding country as nothing has done before in years." President Patterson said it was "the greatest calamity that had ever befallen" the university, and if Smith were not found the school would "bear a lasting mark of shame." (It wasn't mere hyperbole. A professor revealed on October 8 that in the wake of the vanishing, some parents withdrew their children.) R.C. Stoll, a member of the board of trustees, said it was the duty of every student to help find their classmate.

On the morning of October 2, three detectives—accompanied by many faculty members and several hundred UK students—searched the grounds and buildings. They found nothing. But what about that kid's weird boxcar story? Authorities sent telegrams to railroads all over the country, and trainmen scoured many a car, with no results. Railroad authorities pointed out that the boxcars by now had been scattered so widely across the nation that it would be nearly impossible to locate a particular one.

Public anxiety did not lessen with the passing days but rather increased to a fever pitch. President Patterson asked for the formation of a grand jury to investigate. Lexington police were convinced that Smith's classmates knew more than they were telling, a belief UK's faculty refused to consider. The four-professor committee took the curious position that the papers should drop the matter and stop publishing sensational reports.

On October 4, a dispirited Ernest Smith stated on his family's behalf that they believed Willis was dead and that his fellow students were responsible. He said, "I do not believe that I shall ever see him alive again....I feel sure that [students], maybe without intending to, inflicted serious or fatal injuries or disposed of him in some way that has resulted in his death." By this time, a few detectives and UK officials, who previously had been at loggerheads, united in their belief that Willis had left town for his own arcane reasons. However, the vast majority of police officers did not believe it was an intentional disappearance.

On October 5, Ernest Smith's hopes rose when he opened a letter from a woman in Carlisle, Pennsylvania, included a newspaper clipping about a mutilated and incoherent man found in a freight car at Mahoney City on October 2. The abandoned car sat on a siding, just as the popular theory suggested, but the transient turned out to be a thirty-year-old Austrian immigrant.

Inevitably in any missing persons case, publicity-hungry cranks got their hands in, and there were red herrings aplenty. On October 5, police in Decatur, Illinois, received a letter from a writer purporting to be Willis Smith; he wasn't, but credulous souls suggested that the letter was the work of a kidnapping gang that really did have Smith hostage and was writing the letter in a clumsy attempt to trick the police into ending their investigation.

While looking through his missing brother's trunk, Ernest found a letter from a dainty young woman in Tennessee informing Willis that, regrettably, she did not feel a romantic attachment to him. Perhaps Willis had left school to plead with her—or to commit suicide? Police sent her an inquiring telegraph. She confirmed that she did write the rejection letter, but the boy's whereabouts were a mystery to her. (One of the university's professors leaked the letter's discovery to the press, much to Ernest's outrage, since he had insisted on its confidentiality.)

On October 8 came the droll spectacle of Willis Smith being "positively identified" on the same day in locations several hundred miles apart. A railroad conductor was sure he picked up Willis as a passenger at Winchester, Kentucky, while two eagle-eyed clerks and several bellboys at the St. Nicholas Hotel in Decatur, Illinois, spotted Willis applying for a job in their establishment. All were mistaken, but the folks in Decatur insisted for days that they were right.

Someone told Professor A.E. Smith, one of the missing man's brothers, that Willis had surfaced in Ashland, and he traveled all the way there only to find it was a baseless rumor. Ernest made a similarly fruitless trip to Russellville in November.

Amateur detectives offered their services to the Smith family, but of course, they said, they could not be expected to work for free. A fortuneteller dreamed that Smith had drowned in Mulligan Branch, a stream that flowed through campus. A search turned up exactly nothing. A woman living out in the country saw Smith's murder reenacted in a dream, and poor Ernest wasted most of a day driving her from location to location looking for the place she saw in her vision. Searchers uselessly dragged a pond on her say-so.

Stung by the press's implications that UK was a haven for rowdies, on October 5 the senior class offered $25 for information on Smith's whereabouts (to which the university added $100) and published a letter complaining about "the unjust and groundless suspicion of yellow journalism and a prejudiced police force." The junior, sophomore and freshman classes issued like sentiments. The students complained particularly about the *Courier-Journal*'s coverage of the disappearance and tales of student lawlessness, and the paper obligingly fired back in an editorial on October 7:

> [The students] *are naturally presumable to be innocent until proved guilty. But Smith has disappeared; there were pranks on the night of his disappearance; there are rumors. Under the circumstances, there is nothing for any newspaper to do but to chronicle the circumstances. Instead of inveighing against the newspapers for publishing what they choose to call "baseless," but not yet disproved, rumors the members of the faculty of State University were better employed pushing the investigation in every conceivable way rather than discourage it; also, in taking steps to end forever hazing in all its forms.*

A desperate Ernest Smith urged all citizens, in letters published by the *Lexington Evening Gazette* and the *Evening Leader* on October 10, to keep an eye out for Willis. Somebody somewhere must know *something*, he implored. He feared that public interest in the mystery was decreasing.

By October 11, the near-universal opinion of the faculty and students at UK was that Willis Smith intentionally had left town, but many outsiders thought this was just the school's way of deflecting criticism. It was telling that the four classes at the university offered a reward for information about Smith, but each included a clause that the money would not be paid *if* it turned out he disappeared voluntarily. At the end of the month, a Louisville girl who was a student at UK gave frank insider's information to the *Courier-Journal*. She related that the Smith disappearance remained the "principal topic of conversation" on campus but that the faculty and students were still angry at their unflattering depiction by the press. "Everyone there thinks that Smith simply got up and went away and makes fun of the idea that he was bound and gagged and thrown in a boxcar. That story, anyway, originated in the mind of a small boy," she said, adding that those in the know considered the Black Hand letter Ernest Smith received "a howling joke."

The grand jury met on October 14 to plumb the depths of the puzzle. No one had high expectations, since the grand jury had been unable to get straight answers out of the UK students questioned about the Halloween riot of a few years before. The jury questioned President Patterson, faculty members and students but adjourned on October 24 after reaching no conclusion whatsoever.

The Smiths refused to give up, however. Newspapers reported on November 5 that the family had hired a Pinkerton detective, considered among the finest in the nation.

On December 26 came an astonishing and very confident-sounding headline in the *Courier-Journal*: "Smith's Body Lies in Sewer." However, a careful reading of the article revealed that no body had been found and that it was a theory of one of those grand jurors, who insisted on remaining anonymous. He thought that Smith had been disposed of in an eighteen-foot sewer ditch on Winslow Street near campus. He said, "[T]he grand jury was so impressed with this view that they would have had the ditch reopened and searched if the judge had not informed them there were no funds available for this purpose."

What evidence did they found so convincing? Well, it was an unsigned letter to Ernest Smith, written by a woman who said she had stepped outside on the night Willis disappeared. She had overheard an argument among students, one of whom collapsed when another threw a rock at his head, and then she heard this *mildly* incriminating dialogue emanating from the darkness:

"He's dead!"

"You killed him."

"You are as much to blame as I am. Here, let's get him away from here."

The jurors were convinced! In fact, there *had* been an open ditch on Winslow Street on the night of September 22 that laborers completely filled in a few days later. Nevertheless, the night watchman said he had seen no students stashing a corpse, and as it would have cost an estimated $250 to $300 to excavate the ditch, everyone just said the heck with it and let the matter stand. The Smiths found this laissez-faire attitude unsatisfactory and insisted that the grand jury take up the investigation again when it reconvened on January 13, 1909. UK professor A.M. Wilson sarcastically suggested that the Kentucky newspapers, which had been constantly flogging the story of the Smith disappearance—he specifically called out the *Courier-Journal*, the *Lexington Herald* and the *Lexington Leader*—pay for the excavation of the sewer. They could increase their circulation by releasing on-the-spot bulletins from the site, he said. The *Courier-Journal* retorted in a biting editorial that if any people on earth should want to see the mystery solved, it ought to be the faculty at UK.

At the end of the year, UK students started raising funds to have that ditch uncovered. They even offered to do the digging themselves in relay teams. It's a good thing that they neither raised the money nor took shovels in hand because on December 30 a report came that a young wanderer had turned up in Owensboro. It was Willis Smith!

He had reappeared at the Fourteenth Street home of his sister, Mrs. Elmer Hubbard. After he had a long rest, the authorities asked the question that had been on the lips of the entire state for three months: *Where have you been all this time while your family worried themselves sick and the Commonwealth spent untold time and taxpayer money searching for you?* His response was a masterwork of nonsense, a monolith of steaming bovine excrement. It would have taken a squad of the melodramatic novelists of the era to come up with anything equal to it.

On the night of September 23, said Willis, he had left his boardinghouse, not to go to campus as his brother Ernest had reported but to get kindling wood for his room. He had seen four disguised young men of villainous stamp. They had chloroformed him and thrown him into a boxcar. When he revived, the car was moving, and his abductors were standing guard. Sometime later, the four evildoers had turned Smith over to six older men, heavily armed with revolvers and Winchester rifles, who had taken him to northwestern Wisconsin. There they held him captive in a mountain cave. At all times, two men had kept watch over him. Smith noted that they were well dressed and "used good language":

> *"Why do you keep me here?" I would often ask them, but they would not give me any answer. Time and again I told them I had not done anything to any person in the world. They seemed to think that I knew something. On several occasions, they tried to get me to drink drugs. I guess they thought I would talk if I drank what they gave me.... The men did not treat me mean, but when I insisted on asking questions they threatened me.*

Sometimes Smith had gotten two meals a day, sometimes one. Finally, on the night of Monday, December 28, Willis escaped, traveling forty or fifty miles *on foot*—overnight!—to the nearest railroad tracks. He hopped a freight and hoboed his way to his sister's home in Owensboro. Why would anyone go through all this extravagant trouble to kidnap and hold a college kid? Willis shrugged and said he couldn't puzzle that one out either.

Faculty, police, fellow students and the press greeted Willis's story with a universal cry of "Huh?" (Friendly tip for people who consider staging their own disappearance: when you are found, and you probably will be, at least come up with a plausible story.) The *Owensboro Messenger* sneered at Smith's efforts at dramaturgy, calling his yarn "a very artistic piece of work" that was "clumsy in nearly every detail" and adding, "He may have left Lexington in a boxcar, but if so, it was very probably his own voluntary act." The *Courier-Journal* rang in the New Year by remarking, "It is a pity that a youth responsible for such things should have had so little regard for the seriousness of the affair as to come home with a story so flimsy as to proclaim itself at once the wild fabrication of a shallow nature and a dime novel grade of mind."

Still, everyone *was* glad to have him back, especially his rejoicing family and UK's President Patterson, whose staunch belief that Smith had left on his own was vindicated with a whoop. He released a statement: "While, of course, I had no idea from whence he would come, I have felt sure he would eventually turn up safe and well." In some circles, people suggested that Smith's return saved UK's reputation. It also saved many students from getting blisters on their hands, as they were planning to excavate that ditch on campus, but Smith's reemergence the day before spared them the trouble.

On the last day of 1908, Smith fessed up. Skipping town was his own idea, and the reason was that he feared an imminent hazing. "I understood that I was to be hazed the night I disappeared," he explained. "If they attempted to haze me I would have been hurt, or some of the students would have been and that would have involved my brother. So I disappeared." In reality, he had taken a train to Cincinnati and from there to Wisconsin, where he had worked at a lumber camp. Then he was a cook and waiter in a Chinese restaurant in Bloomington, Illinois. At last, he had decided that enough was enough and came home to Kentucky. However, Smith vowed that he would not re-enroll at UK. If the hazers had wanted to give him a hard time back in September, he would have been an absolutely irresistible target now.

However, the students got back at Smith in another, more creative way. As the first-year anniversary of the non-vanishing approached, some of his former classmates built a mock grave in the dark of night, on which they placed a tombstone: "Gone but not forgotten. Erected in memory of our departed brother Willis E. Smith, who so mysteriously disappeared on the 21st of September, 1908. Erected by the Class of 1912." Two years later, on September 22, 1911, the senior class held a faux funeral complete with pallbearers, a coffin and (one assumes) suitably lugubrious music from the university band. The class president delivered a eulogy, and the students responded with a raucous school chant. The coffin's inscription read, "W.E. Smith, departed September 22, '08." Because he *did* depart, in a way!

I think UK students should revive the tradition of honoring Willis Smith every September 22, but without cutting electric lines or stripping cops.

OVER THE YEARS, IT was called "Louisville's most intriguing mystery" and its "most bizarre mystery." The whole thing started like a real-life Agatha Christie story.

Ella McDowell Rogers lived in no. 14 at the Baringer Manor Apartments. Her husband, Hamilton Rogers, circulation manager for the *Louisville Herald-Post*, died in an auto crash in March 1927. At only twenty-nine years old, Ella was a very attractive and well-to-do widow.

On Sunday, October 7, 1928, she returned from a trip to Chicago. She had a guest that evening: Hal Harned, a banker from Dawson Springs and friend of the family. He later told authorities that something unusual happened during his visit:

> *I spent the early part of the evening with Mrs. Rogers in her apartment.... While I was there the lights went out suddenly. I think it was a little before 8 o'clock. We supposed a fuse had blown out and I offered to go to the basement and help find the trouble. But Mrs. Rogers said she wasn't afraid to go and preferred to go alone. So I left in a taxicab. Mrs. Rogers told me she was going to a movie theater in the neighborhood. She was in the best of spirits and assured me that she was not afraid to be left alone.*

Harned had left around 8:30 p.m. He said he had called Mrs. Rogers from Louisville's Central Station at 10:00 p.m. that night but got no answer, but then he remembered that she mentioned that she was going to the movies. She probably disappeared during the hour and a half between his departure from her apartment and his follow-up phone call.

A week passed without a sign of Ella Rogers. Her roommate, Lorraine Smith, was staying temporarily with an aunt while Smith's uncle was out of town. Several times, she had called Rogers but received no answer. Around October 14, Smith let herself in with her key and found the place deserted. She noticed that none of Rogers's clothing was missing, and the trunks she had taken on her Chicago trip were still unpacked.

Also around the fourteenth, Ella's father-in-law, Ira Rogers, concerned that she might be sick, asked the apartment's custodian, Philip Haynes, to check on her. Haynes said he had to climb through a window to get in.

There was no trace of Ella, reported Haynes, but the table was set with the remains of a very cold and stale chicken salad dinner still on the plates.

Ira Rogers wanted to keep news of the disappearance out of the papers, and for five weeks, few people knew about it other than the widow's closest friends and Chief of Detectives M. Rey Yarberry. However, the story leaked out and hit the front page of the papers on November 17. The family's desire for secrecy is understandable; likely, they didn't want idle speculation to run rampant, and potential embarrassment could be spared if Ella turned up on her own, as most missing persons do. It is hard to deny that the long delay between the disappearance and the public acknowledgment of the fact probably did more harm than good. Who can say how many clues and leads were lost in the interval?

The clues were scarce indeed by mid-November. No one who knew Ella considered her depressed or suicidal. Yarberry determined that she had left her apartment with neither hat nor coat, nor jewelry nor money, and wearing her oldest dress. Yarberry assumed that she either had met with foul play or took flight while under the influence of amnesia, a condition we now call a dissociative fugue state. However, Yarberry admitted that he had no firm evidence to support either conclusion. Perhaps she had disappeared voluntarily? It seemed unlikely. There had been no recent withdrawals from her bank account, and her safe deposit box had been untouched since July.

On November 20, Commonwealth's Attorney W. Clarke Otte launched a personal investigation into the mystery, in hopes of finding enough evidence to form a grand jury. Even the powers bestowed upon Otte were useless in uncovering much more than unsubstantiated rumors. An attorney who lived in the same apartment building remembered hearing "three distinct screams" coming from the area behind it but was not sure if October 7 was the correct date. Supposedly, a man from Chicago called "Mac" visited Mrs. Rogers often, but he was never identified nor located.

Suspicions settled on custodian Philip Haynes—whether because he said and did shifty things, because he had a criminal record, merely because he was black or a combination of all these factors is anyone's guess. Haynes protested that he was barely acquainted with Mrs. Rogers. He had only worked in Baringer Manor for a few months, he said, and the young widow was gone most of that time. He stated that he always stayed at his house on Sunday nights, not in his quarters at the Baringer; his wife, Leila, said that he was at home with her all the evening of October 7. On November 20, Haynes first provoked detectives' curiosity when he gave them a discursive recounting about his whereabouts on the night Rogers disappeared. So nervous was he that, according to one account, he "fairly shouted" his story: "I'm telling you everything I know! I don't see why you keep coming to me to explain where that woman went!" He contradicted himself several times as to the time he left work on October 7, but that may be understandable considering the lapse of several weeks.

Not so easy to explain: Haynes swore that he did not have a key to Rogers's apartment, hence his entrance to the place via a window when asked to investigate. However, when he quit his job at Baringer Manor, he turned in his key ring to the apartment's new custodian, George Adams, who told detectives that one of the keys opened Rogers's door. Adams said custodians were not allowed to have keys to individual apartments in the first place, as residents were expected to telephone if they needed a service. So why did Haynes have a key? (In fact, Mrs. Rogers's own key and a little purse in which she kept it were the only two items known to be missing from her apartment.) Furthermore, Adams doubted that Ella Rogers meant it seriously when she told Harned she would fix the fuse since all she had to do was call a custodian to have it repaired.

The apartment's basement contained a laundry, garages, storage lockers and the janitor's quarters. Authorities futilely searched all of these locations for bloodstains or any of Ella Rogers's property. They even searched the ashes in the incinerator.

There were two developments on November 22, the forty-sixth day after the widow's disappearance. After further questioning Philip Haynes, detectives found discrepancies in his story. They didn't give specific details to the press but noted that the inconsistences involved the state of the apartment when he first entered it and something about the fuse box. (Some information leaked to the press: later newspaper articles revealed that the fuse had been unscrewed but not burned out, suggesting that someone manually loosened it rather than the fuse having blown.) Police arrested Haynes. There was a legitimate reason for holding him: he had shot at another man in a poolroom during a botched robbery on April 16, 1927, and afterward failed to show up for his court date. A bench warrant had been issued for his arrest, but it was not served until he was connected with the Rogers mystery. Yarberry assured the press that Haynes's arrest "had nothing to do with the Rogers case," and technically speaking, it didn't. Yet it is hard to escape the feeling that the police were glad to have a reason for keeping Haynes in the slammer just in case evidence in the disappearance pointed in his direction.

On the same day, banker Hal Harned, the last person known to see Mrs. Rogers alive, arrived from Dawson Springs for a police interview. A check with a taxi company proved that he had in fact called for a cab at 8:35 p.m. on October 7, just as he had said. The driver, who had gone into Baringer Manor to pick up his fare, confirmed another part of Harned's story: the cabby said the apartment's lights were out. Rumor held that Mrs. Rogers had asked Harned to leave the apartment after she received a mysterious phone call, but the banker denied it. He spoke with a reporter but was distinctly unwilling to talk about the case, answering most questions with variations on the phrase, "I simply do not care to discuss that." Perhaps he felt guilty about leaving Rogers alone in a darkened room with such disastrous consequences.

On November 23, investigator dragged the lake in Cherokee Park, which was located next to the Baringer Manor Apartments, as a deeply interested crowd watched. Searchers also checked sewers, sinkholes and creeks. Result of all this hard work: bupkis. Desperate to scare up some leads, the *Courier-Journal* and the *Louisville Times* offered a $500 reward for information leading to the discovery of Ella Rogers, alive or dead, and another $500 for information leading to the conviction of her murderer, if murdered she was.

A woman had committed suicide by poisoning at an Elkhart, Indiana hotel on October 17. She had cut all the labels off her clothing to prevent easy identification, but some said she resembled the missing widow. Rogers's father-in-law studied a photo of the dead woman and said that while the resemblance was close, it wasn't her. In all, six of Ella's relatives and friends examined the photo and denied that it was her. Their belief was confirmed when a dentist sent a description of Ella's teeth to Elkhart and investigators found no match.

Suspicions against Haynes gained traction when two young girls complained that he had sexually harassed them. One lived at Hilmar Apartments, where Haynes previously had worked, and the other lived at Baringer Manor. Detectives also found that Haynes had lied when he said he had resigned from his job at the Baringer. Rather, the owners fired him. He had also claimed that he used to work for the Pullman Car Company, but a few phone calls exposed that lie as well. Haynes insisted that he was being railroaded:

> All that at the Hilmar was explained away satisfactorily to everybody. I know nothing about any complaint against me at the Baringer Manor. Anyone saying anything like that against me is telling a lie....I know nothing about the lady's disappearance and have no theory on the case. You know a mastermind was behind it. If detectives and newspapermen cannot figure it out, how could I? Anything that happened was planned with lots of brains and money.

The custodian's attorney, Clifford Dye, told the press, "It is evident they are holding Haynes on account of the Rogers case, and not because of the old charges." He was probably right.

The search for the widow went high tech on November 25, when radio stations broadcast appeals for information all over America. No leads were uncovered, but the next day investigators took a close look at a pile of cinders intended for sidewalk construction that originally had come from the air chamber of the furnace in the Baringer Manor basement. After sifting through the notably foul-smelling ashes, they found an object that appeared to be the leather heel from a woman's shoe and "a handful of small, chalky bits of a substance." Were they pieces of cremated human bones? Ella's brother, Wallace McDowell, thought they were—he had some authority in the matter, as he was a Cincinnati undertaker. George Adams, current Baringer custodian, confirmed that dinner scraps containing bones were not disposed of in the furnace. At the same time, another intriguing find turned up in the basement: a broken monkey wrench stained with what appeared to be blood. Detectives guarded the bone fragments and the wrench for testing.

It developed that other apartment residents had heard those aforementioned three screams. Some confirmed that they had heard the noise on the night of October 7; some thought that the sounds seemed to be coming from the basement! Charles Lanfrom said he had been determined to investigate, but his frightened wife had begged him not to go, assuring him, "It's *just* the janitor beating his wife." (!?) At this late date, of course, we cannot be sure if they really heard screams on the same night as the widow's disappearance or if it was a manifestation of the all-too-human tendency to remember thrilling details after the fact whether they happened or not.

Mrs. Lanfrom told detectives that the morning after she and her husband heard those screams, she asked custodian Haynes if he had heard them too. "What time did you hear them?" he asked.

"About 8:30 Sunday night."

"I didn't hear them because I left and didn't come back until 11:30."

If Mrs. Lanfrom's memory was correct, Haynes's statement was most interesting. Several days previously, he had told detectives that he *never* stayed at the Baringer on Sunday nights. He was lying either to the police or to Mrs. Lanfrom.

On November 30, chemist Dr. Vernon Robins started analyzing the putative bone fragments, the alleged shoe heel, grate bars from the apartment furnace and the monkey wrench. From the start, there were doubts about the wrench's value as a clue. Detectives found it in a tool chest in the apartment's basement, and it was difficult to believe that someone with sense and foresight enough to clean up a crime scene would be so stupid as to stash the wrench in a place where it was certain to be found, and uncleaned at that. Why not just dispose of it?

The doubts were well founded. On December 1, Dr. Robins announced that there was "nothing startling" in his examination of the wrench. Two days later, he stated that the grates, the ashes, the chalky substance and the heel-like object were all worthless: "I have found no evidence of any value in any of the articles of materials brought to the laboratory in the Rogers case."

The embarrassments for law enforcement just kept coming. Detectives received a tip that "around October 10," someone spotted "two Negroes" clandestinely digging a grave behind the Christian Church in Middletown.

Louisville detectives made a hasty trip to Middletown and soon discovered that the rightful occupant of the plot was the late Mr. Pleas Clarkston, age sixty-nine, who had died at the county poorhouse on October 12. His sons had buried him, and it was in no way a dark secret, as the elders of Christian Church had sanctioned it. At least the detectives found out the truth before breaking out the shovels.

On December 3, boys at play uncovered a shallow grave while digging in the Indian Hills subdivision. Hopes rose that Ella Rogers had been found at last, until coroner Roy Carter determined that the skeleton was that of a large black woman who died at least fifteen years before. Strangely, fresh leaves were nestled among the buried bones, indicating that an industrious ghoul recently had exhumed the body at another location and reburied it at the subdivision. Some pieces of skull did not match the skeleton, indicating that the original faraway grave had held two bodies. Police never identified the skeleton(s), making the discovery yet another minor satellite mystery attached to the Rogers disappearance.

Philip Haynes was released from jail on December 4, and the two detectives given the task of finding out what happened to Ella Rogers were reassigned to other cases. In fact, authorities more or less called off the investigation that day, admitting that they had worked every possible clue to its limit and were defeated unless something new turned up.

Abruptly on December 21, police rearrested Haynes on that indictment of malicious shooting from 1927 and held him under a $2,000 bond. Investigators reopened the Rogers disappearance the next day. Police were close-mouthed as to new evidence, but the press noted that chemist Dr. Robins had made a personal visit to the Baringer Manor Apartments back on December 10 and 11.

Officials at the Frankfort Reformatory declared that Haynes's real name was Harry Watkins, alias Pete Watkins, and that they had mug shots to prove it. While waiting in his cell for further developments, Haynes decided that he had better be honest about his past. He admitted that the jail officials' charge was correct. On November 17, 1914, he had been incarcerated on a charge of housebreaking. Release came on October 11, 1920, but two months later he got in trouble for parole violation. He was arrested for another burglary on October 27, 1924, and went back to the reformatory a month later. Haynes declared that he was sure he would go back to prison for at least four years, for parole violation if for no other reason.

The new evidence in the case was unveiled on January 5, 1929: whoever cleaned up the basement of the Baringer didn't do as thorough a job as investigators previously thought. Blood had leaked through cracks in the concrete floor near the furnace. Dr. Robins's task was to find if it was human. A pair of Philip Haynes's shoes also bore smears of something that seemed to be blood.

As Dr. Robins performed his tests and Haynes stewed in his cell, major excitement unfolded when a body floated up in Beargrass Creek in Cherokee Park on February 16. The Baringer Manor Apartments overlooked Cherokee Park, and many did not think that coincidental. A crowd of hundreds gathered as the corpse was collected. So important was the discovery considered that, according to the *Courier-Journal*, "fully a score of policemen, detectives, and motorcycle patrolmen hurried to the park." Conventional wisdom held that Mrs. Rogers was missing no longer. However, the "floater" turned out to be Mrs. Bessie Mahoney, age forty-five, missing since January 16. As soon as word spread that it wasn't Mrs. Rogers, the disappointed onlookers went their separate ways and returned to their activities.

On February 23, police again questioned Philip Haynes, perhaps hoping this time they would get lucky and hear a confession. The papers described it as a planned "final grilling" and a "last concerted effort," but it lasted merely forty-five minutes. The results, if any, were kept secret, but the brevity of the meeting suggests they didn't learn much.

By 1929, it was possible for scientists to distinguish between human and animal blood by applying the Uhlenhuth serum test, developed in 1900. The substance found in the Baringer Manor basement floor was blood, but its origin must never have been determined since newspaper accounts are flatly contradictory. Some declare that it was human, while others state that the results were inconclusive. Perhaps the blood was too badly deteriorated to make a positive result possible. In any case, at this point investigators surrendered all hope of proving Haynes a murderer.

On May 3, authorities sent the custodian to the Frankfort Reformatory for violating his parole. He was supposed to serve out the remainder of his term, four years and four months, but instead he was paroled on July 26 after the state Board of Charities and Corrections determined that he had not violated his first parole that was granted him in October 1920 after all.

The investigation ended with a whimper rather than a bang—in fact, several whimpers. In March 1930, the proprietors of the Baringer Manor successfully sued the estate of Ella Rogers for back rent. The Rogers disappearance made Kentucky legal history: because of the case, the legislature passed a law providing for a curator to handle the affairs of missing persons.

A year later, a story made the rounds that Mrs. Rogers had been murdered and buried near Seatonville. Chief of Police Ratcliffe described the yarn as a "wild rumor" and said that it wasn't worth investigating. Posterity does not record the details of the story, nor the reasons why Ratcliffe dismissed it out of hand.

Ella's brother, Wallace, reported in October 1935 that he still received harassing calls from opportunistic cranks threatening to harm his sister if he failed to pay a ransom—as though kidnappers still would be holding her after seven years. The missing widow was declared legally dead on October 11, 1935.

On August 24, 1937, railroad workers found parts of a woman's skeleton buried near the tracks a mile and a half from Buechel. Some briefly surmised that it was Ella until a dental comparison proved otherwise.

Philip Haynes died of tuberculosis in a New York hospital on January 6, 1947, vowing to the end that he knew nothing about the disappearance. A few weeks after his death, the Louisville police received an anonymous package containing Ella's handwritten will and newspaper articles about the mystery. An inquiry showed that a Louisville woman, Mrs. James Dewboys, discovered the will and the clippings in a 1929 issue of *True Detective* magazine that her husband found in a scrap pile. The magazine included an article about Rogers's disappearance. Mrs. Dewboys thought she should send these items to the police but claimed to know nothing about their provenance. She sent them anonymously out of fear that she would be hassled if she included her name.

In 1957, Lieutenant Charles Young, then the head of Louisville Police Department's Homicide Squad, acknowledged that although he had worked on many crimes, Rogers's vanishing—which occurred before Young joined the force—exerted a special fascination. "It's still the most interesting case of all to me," he said.

So what *actually* happened to Ella Rogers? We will never know in this lifetime, but the answer that best seems to fit the circumstances is that the police were on the right track all along and the custodian murdered her. To summarize and speculate:

Haynes had a history of harassing women and violence (such as the shooting at the pool hall and, perhaps, wife-beating). He contradicted himself repeatedly when speaking with detectives. He had a key to Rogers's apartment, which he was not supposed to have, and lied about it. The loosened fuse to Rogers's apartment was located in the basement, where Haynes had private living quarters. Likely, he unscrewed the fuse, and when

Rogers couldn't contact him by phone she went downstairs to fix it herself, whereupon he killed her. He told conflicting stories about his whereabouts on the night of October 7: at various times he said he was at home with his wife all night, that he went to church or that he returned to the Baringer at 11:30 p.m. Investigators found a quantity of blood in the basement; if not human it must have been from an animal, and neither Haynes nor anyone else explained how so much animal blood could have turned up in such an improbable place.

Assuming Haynes was the killer, how he disposed of the body is a minor mystery within the major mystery. Contrary to the theory of contemporary detectives, he probably did not put it in the furnace. Total cremation requires far higher temperatures than one can get from an ordinary furnace, and burning corpses smell bad—*very* bad—so it beggars belief that no apartment residents noticed. However, if the custodian were also a killer, he had plenty of time to hide the body and clean up since Rogers's disappearance caused no major concern for a week. It sounds very much as though the authorities had a gut feeling that Philip Haynes was responsible for the disappearance but could never find enough evidence to prove it. Of course, one can come up with imaginative, plausible alternate scenarios. Perhaps some other resident of Baringer Manor, knowing that the custodian would be gone Sunday night, loosened the fuse to lure Ella down to the basement. However, that wouldn't explain Haynes's lies and contradictions or the fact that he flouted the rules by having the key to her apartment.

It's a mystery that resonates after nearly a century.

DON'T GIVE UP THE DAY JOB

Alvin "Shipwreck" Kelly became a quasi-celebrity in the 1920s for performing crazy public stunts, particularly flagpole sitting, in various American cities. On May 20, 1928, he was in Louisville, engaged in sitting on a pole for one hundred hours. However, there are far worse ways to become notorious than flagpole sitting, such as electric chair sitting.

On this particular morning, as Kelly was impressing goggle-eyed spectators across town, sixty-four-year-old carpenter William A. Muse of 132 East Gray Street traveled on a streetcar with someone he thought was a friend. Destination: St. Louis Cemetery. There Muse bent over to lay a bouquet on the grave of his wife, Annie, who had died in 1922, a ritual he performed every Sunday. His so-called friend sneaked up behind him and hit him several times in the head with a hammer. The attacker took $1,020 from Muse's pocket and fled.

Another visitor found Muse staggering about the grounds and helped him to the home of cemetery superintendent George Brandt. Before falling unconscious, Muse asked a bystander to place the flowers on his wife's plot and said that his attacker was a young acquaintance, Ballard Ratcliffe.

The police considered that a darn good clue and sent out an all-points bulletin for this Mr. Ratcliffe, whom they found slightly over six hours later. Thirty-nine-year-old Ratcliffe, formerly of Stone, Pike County, was an insurance agent; he couldn't have been worse at his trade than he was at murder, at which he proved to be totally incompetent across the board. When

he saw detectives and police officers approaching, he impulsively shouted, "My God! He isn't dying, is he?"—a statement that would prove none too easy to explain away later. He had $626 in his pocket, which was considered suspicious since he wasn't exactly affluent; in fact, he roomed at the YMCA because he couldn't afford an apartment. Naturally, the detectives wanted to know why he had hundreds of dollars on his person.

"Why, I won the money at the racetrack yesterday," protested a rattled Ratcliffe. Of course, the authorities easily could have gone to the racetrack to check out his alibi. However, this proved unnecessary.

"Yeah? What was the name of the horse you bet on? What were the odds?" asked the detectives.

After a long, instructive pause, Ratcliffe replied, "I dunno."

Officers hurried him off to Muse's room at St. Anthony's Hospital, where the victim readily identified him, and Ratcliffe probably wished he were sitting on a flagpole somewhere far, far away. He very unwisely asked

Sergeant Odios Hazel, "Can they convict someone on the testimony of a semi-conscious man?"

Detectives visited the boardinghouse where Muse lived. The proprietress said that he frequently took meals there with a Ballard Ratcliffe lookalike who happened to be an insurance salesman, also like Ratcliffe.

An inspection of St. Louis Cemetery revealed that Ratcliffe carelessly left his blood-smeared weapon six feet from the grave and had dropped a business card just outside the gates. Not only that, a witness saw a man answering to Ratcliffe's description running out of the graveyard just after the time of the attack. Some witnesses saw Ratcliffe getting off a streetcar near the cemetery; others saw Ratcliffe and Muse walking together to that location. The assault was so public that the best one could say in Ratcliffe's defense was that it was performed in the heat of the moment rather than premeditatedly. But then, who casually brings a hammer to a cemetery?

So far, Ratcliffe could be charged with assault, attempted murder, theft and probably a few other things as well. When Mr. Muse died on May 23, all those lesser crimes were overshadowed. When formally charged in court, all Ratcliffe could say was, "I know they've got me charged with a pretty serious crime, but I didn't do it. Just tell everybody for me that I am not guilty."

While Ratcliffe waited to go on trial, the Fidelity and Columbia Trust Company, administrators of Muse's estate, slapped him with a lawsuit for the money he stole. Then Ratcliffe's own lawyer, Thurman Dixon, sued him when he failed to pay the agreed-upon fee.

When the trial began on June 25, Ratcliffe's defense attorneys, E.B. Gabbard and Mr. Dixon—presumably Ratcliffe paid him—intended to enter an insanity plea. This idea died a flaming death when a panel of doctors testified that they found no trace of madness in the defendant.

Ratcliffe did not take the stand to testify on his own behalf, which is a Constitutional right but also generally a pretty good sign that defense lawyers know their client is guilty and are afraid to put him on. Not only that, his attorneys offered what we would now call a plea bargain, saying that they would enter a guilty plea if Ratcliffe would get a life sentence. They also asked that the jury not hear sordid details of the crime, which, they worried, would make the defendant look unsympathetic. Commonwealth's Attorney W. Clarke Otte refused to consider the offers.

Ratcliffe got some cold comfort on June 27 when the jury was deadlocked. That is to say, it agreed unanimously that he was guilty but could not get together on the appropriate punishment. Eight wanted him to get the

chair, while four advocated prison for life. The refusal to agree meant that Ratcliffe would go on trial again.

The second trial began on December 6, 1928. All of the aforementioned circumstances were brought out, as related by well over a dozen witnesses. The defense could muster up only two witnesses. Reporters noted that Ratcliffe could not bring himself to look at the bloody hammer brought in as evidence.

In the face of all this, it was no surprise when the jury gave Ratcliffe the death sentence on December 7 after deliberating for less than an hour and a half. The date was set for February 11, 1929, but later changed to June 13, the net effect of which was to give Ratcliffe three more months to consider what he had done and take what comfort he could find in philosophy.

Governor Flem Sampson took time out of his busy schedule to proclaim, "It is beyond the conception of the human mind that a man could become so depraved as to take the life of a friend at such a solemn moment and for no other reason than to obtain a few paltry dollars. This was the premeditated, deliberately planned action of a mind distorted by greed and avarice." The heated statement undoubtedly cost the governor Ratcliffe's vote.

Engineers at Eddyville Prison tested the electric chair on June 10. Ratcliffe spent his final days writing a massive eighty-page letter to his elderly mother. For a while, he shammed insanity by maintaining a glum silence but finally dropped the pretense. When a reporter asked him near the end if he were guilty or innocent, he replied:

> *I have told my story, now you fellows print it and let it be a lesson. If you find yourself unprepared when you come to die, it will be a much more terrible thing than what faces me. I am prepared. I have been praying four times a day. I don't dread to die one bit. I am glad to die. I hate to leave my wife and girlie—she's just 16—sisters and brothers and mother. I thought it was God's plan that I should escape the chair in this way* [faking insanity, that is] *and if it hadn't been for that talk with the chaplain this morning I'd have done it. Don't blame me. If one of you fellows were in this cell you'd have done anything to get free.*

Still, he steadfastly refused to admit guilt or innocence and sidestepped the question every time someone asked.

Ratcliffe went to the chair early in the morning of June 13, paving the way for another man who went after him. The governor gave three black men also scheduled for the chair stays of execution.

According to death penalty historian Daniel Allen Hearn, Ratcliffe's capital crime was considered so repugnant that anti–death penalty zealots dared not support him: "The American Society for the Abolition of Capital Punishment…apparently wrote Ratcliffe off as being bad for business" and sought more affable murderers to shed tears over.

BLUE GOON OF KENTUCKY

Every once in a while, a community is plagued by an intangible being that seems to be a cross between the strictly material and the purely imaginary. Hence, Spring-Heel Jack in Victorian London…the Mad Gasser, who supposedly terrorized Mattoon, Illinois, in 1944…the Phantom Prowler of Baltimore's O'Donnell Heights in 1951…and the focus of our story, the Blue Man of Louisville, Kentucky. If the story isn't entirely true, it ought to be.

The indigo intruder first turned up near Eighth and Oak Streets in the winter of 1921. People saw it, or him, chiefly between Sixth and Eighth Streets and the adjoining streets of Kentucky, Oak and Breckinridge. By January 17, the thing had become such a topic of nervous conversation in that area of the city that the *Louisville Courier-Journal* took front-page notice. A drugstore clerk swore that the Blue Man wore bulletproof armor. Reese Carrell told the reporter that he had seen the Blue Man outside his family's home at 1011 South Eighth Street and that it was no ghost: "I've only been knocked down once in my life, and it did it." Carrell explained, "It's been around here every night for the last two weeks. What it's after, I don't know. But one night last week when I came home at about 11 o'clock, I saw somebody standing on our front step. I thought it was my father, and I walked right up to him. 'Looking for the Blue Man, Pop?' I asked him, and just then, he hit me in the chest. I was knocked against the fence, and when I got up it was gone." Reese was one of the few to get a good look at the cerulean stranger; he confirmed that the man was over six feet tall and had a blue face.

The next night, the Blue Man broke into the Carrell residence by opening the shutters and placing a washtub under the window. He left after stealing the family patriarch's pants. Night after that, young Reese Carrell lay in wait with a shotgun. Hearing a noise, he ran outside and saw the Blue Man standing in the neighbor's backyard, twenty-five feet away. Carrell fired at the blue burglar, who leaped unhurt over a fence. A few nights later, Carrell took another shot at him, and again he vanished, although a coal shed received a load of buckshot as collateral damage.

Carrell's father took a shot at the Blue Man next time he appeared. "I never missed a rabbit or a bird in my life," he told the *Courier-Journal* reporter. "But the shots went right through him."

"Do you think it's a ghost?" asked the reporter.

"Ghost? What would a ghost want with my pants?" demanded Mr. Carrell, who clearly had no use for metaphysics. "Here's my idea about spirits. If a man dies and goes to heaven, he doesn't want to come back. If he goes to hell he can't!"

The Blue Man paid un-neighborly calls to every house between 1009 and 1017 South Eighth Street, but a woman told the *Courier-Journal* reporter that he had made a nightly habit of looking into the window of an elderly sick man, Albert Fogel, who lived at 1017 South Eighth Street. "It's a terrible thing to behold, and the inside of its mouth is all blue," remarked the helpful woman.

Naturally, the reporter sought out Fogel, who confirmed that shortly after the New Year dawned, he was disturbed by the appearance of a "blue and terrible" face, whose possessor would press it against the window. "I was lying awake," he remembered. "All at once three shafts of light came through the shutters. They were the color of the flame you see in the stove there. They stayed several minutes and then disappeared." A few nights later, he heard someone rattling his window shutters as though trying to get inside. Disturbingly, the window rattling continued for several nights, but the would-be invader was unable to enter.

Fogel had a witness: a young relative was present at one of the Blue Man's earliest appearances. She saw him in the yard and ran to him, thinking it to be her father. The figure "disappeared into the darkness."

Mr. Fogel's unwanted visitor showed up every night for two weeks, always between the hours of 7:00 p.m. and 9:00 p.m., so the family lay in wait for him. They would run outside when they saw his leering visage but could never catch him. They took shots at him, but the bullets struck nothing. Fogel's son, Clarence, said that he surprised the Blue Man at 4:30 a.m. one morning: "I ran in the house, got my revolver, and ran out again. It was still there. I wasn't twenty feet away when I fired directly at its body. It ran through the backyard and disappeared."

On the second night of the Blue Man's appearance, the Fogels called for help, which arrived in the form of fifteen policemen, five detectives and two military policemen. The strange visitor eluded this veritable squad.

One night, the family dog barked at the Blue Man, who responded in a fashion that would not draw plaudits from the ASPCA. According to the elder Fogel, "If it's a ghost, it's a strong one, for it kicked the little dog up against our house so hard that he almost came through."

Blue Man sightings came in a variety of incidents that ranged from silly to genuinely creepy. Whether they were crude practical jokes, the effects of mass hysteria, genuine sightings or a combination of all these possibilities, it is now impossible to say. Mrs. Earl Schubnell was enjoying life in her home at 1013 South Eighth on the night of January 13 when she glanced into the kitchen and saw a hand reaching through a broken windowpane. The hand grabbed a curtain and pulled it back. The hand was white, not blue, and its owner ran away after Mrs. Schubnell pierced the air with a healthy scream. Her boarder, Virgil Hobbs, claimed to have seen the neighborhood terror several times and said that he wore a black overcoat and a soft black hat. In fact, said Hobbs, whenever the Blue Man was shot at and escaped, a large white man who dressed like him would usually turn up several minutes later and join the crowd of gawkers attracted by the noise and excitement. Was it the Blue Man out of disguise, mingling with bystanders and secretly enjoying the chaos he had created?

On the night of January 15, the Blue Man peeped through the windows of the Fogels' next-door neighbor, Ben Brocking of 1015 South Eighth.

A jittery populace called the police of the Sixth District several times to check out Blue Man sightings. One officer fired seven shots at the figure at close range, to no discernible effect. On the night of January 18, an auto loaded with police hurried to Eighth and Kentucky to investigate an appearance. By the time they got there, he was gone, but the vicinity was full of citizen posses scanning alleys and backyards. Nobody found clues.

On January 19, while searching the streets for the Blue Man, police arrested Stewart Graven, who had stolen $1,500 worth of merchandise from the American Railway Express Company. Graven, who lived at 738 West Kentucky Street—around the corner from the Carrells' house—had been fired from the company a few days previously, and he swore that he stole the material only so he could feed his wife and baby. Some detectives were convinced that Graven was none other than the Blue Man. From his jail cell, Graven plaintively said, "Me the Blue Man? I wish I was. If I was I wouldn't be in here now!" However, the sightings continued.

Gradually, the Blue Man started doing his thing—whatever "his thing" possibly could have been—on streets outside his usual base of operations. Outside voices irritated Emma Perkins as she tried to sleep on the night of January 16 in her house at 718 Magazine Street. The next night, she saw someone looking in her window like a garden variety Peeping Tom. He was gone when she opened the door. On January 19, her boarder, Stuart Friend, heard someone raising a window and saw a face pressed against the pane. Friend's revolver was unloaded, otherwise he might have ended the Blue Man mystery then and there. The next night, he was prepared. He fired directly at the figure in the window and saw it fall against the fence. Friend and Emma Perkins, firing her own gun, ran outside and found the body gone, like in the conclusion of the movie *Halloween*. The fence bore bullet holes, but there were no traces of blood.

Henry Etzel of 115 South Preston Street was reading the newspaper on the night of January 21 when he heard a light tapping on his door—or, as Poe wrote in "The Raven," Etzel heard "one gently rapping, rapping at my chamber door." He looked outside and saw no one. Etzel went back to his paper. More tapping—this time louder than before. Etzel investigated again; nobody at the door. Back to the paper. More knocking—this time *much* louder. Etzel checked for the third time. Nobody! Etzel was determined to catch the miscreant next time. He did not have long to wait. Shortly came the sound of someone kicking—*kicking!*—the door. Etzel sprang and flung the door open "before the noise died away." He saw no raven, no Blue Man and no neighborhood brat. He did find a heartwarming, friendly letter: "I will call again. Don't be afraid. Your friend, the 'Blue Man,' till we meet again."

On the night of January 22, the unnerving sounds of a turning knob and a creaking door awakened Mrs. L.I. Dilly of 948 South Fifth Street. She alerted the woman in the neighboring apartment, and as they fled the building, they saw a man jumping the back fence. Corporal H.C. Griffin and patrolman E.T. Thornberry fruitlessly searched the house and found no footprints in the backyard, even though the earth was soft. The police left and Mrs. Dilly returned home. Fifteen minutes later, she called again, pleading for the officers to return; she had again been disturbed by someone fiddling with her doorknob. In short order, she saw a face pressed against her window. This time, Mrs. Dilly had a pistol at the ready, and when the form

left the window, she gave pursuit. She tried to shoot the running figure, but the gun didn't fire. By this time, Griffin and Thornberry were back on the scene; again they searched and found no clue. They left, as before, and Mrs. Dilly returned to bed for the third time on that memorable night. She made sure that the gun would fire if she needed it.

Griffin and Thornberry had barely made it back to the station when Mrs. Dilly phoned. The stranger was staring through her window again. The two policemen hurried back with two additional officers. Meanwhile, Mrs. Dilly had chased the Blue Man and fired at him. It seemed that she hit him—she heard someone crying "Oh, oh!" When the four officers arrived, they again found no trace of the intruder, not even a footprint nor blood nor bullet holes. When Mrs. Dilly and the police went inside, she found that someone or some*thing* had moved a glass of water on a table near her bed. She was convinced that the Blue Man had gotten inside after all.

By the end of January, people were so afraid of encountering the Blue Man that juveniles were keeping off the streets at night. However, it seems that the Blue Man—if he were not simply a figment of mass hysteria— had exhausted his diabolical creativity. Instead of scaring people by being a bulletproof voyeur and a stealer of old men's trousers, he was reduced to ringing people's doorbells and disappearing. One would like to think that paranormal creatures have better things to do with their time than play "ding dong ditch" and that lame and unoriginal practical jokers were stealing the Blue Man's thunder.

After January, no one saw Louisville's Blue Man again. Nevertheless, in early February, a large bugaboo in a blue coat and a black hat petrified three women living in the Richter Apartments at Oak and Main. This being would knock on apartment doors and request a drink of water. The residents were not certain if it was male or female, but reporters eager to pump a little more life into a dead story referred to it as the Blue Woman. Folks with a romantic streak might enjoy thinking that Louisville's lonely Blue Man met a woman of the same hue and eloped with her, hence the disappearance of both, and they went to some Blue Heaven to celebrate a Blue Marriage and breed little Blue Babies.

Nevertheless, if present-day residents of this particular section of Louisville happen to see a tall blue man loitering in their backyards or peeking in their windows—and if the Blue Man Group happens not to be in town—they might have reason to be worried. Should the fellow ever turn up in Lexington, the phrase "Go big blue" might take on a new meaning.

SOME MOTHER'S BOY

Tramps—even very young ones—passing through small towns were a common sight in the early twentieth century. Therefore, nobody in Georgetown paid particular attention to a teenage vagrant hanging around the train depot on the night of April 1, 1921. Perhaps some people noticed that he looked well fed and his clothing was in good repair, as though he had not been traveling very many days. Then the teenager, oblivious to danger, crossed the tracks as a train approached. To the horror of onlookers, the train struck him on the head. He died at Ford Memorial Hospital a few hours later.

The sheriff tried to discover the tramp's identity so his family could be alerted and he could be sent home, but he carried no identification. The best the authorities could do was notify the newspapers about the unknown youth who had been killed in their community. They provided a description of his clothing and general appearance, noting that he seemed about seventeen years old; was five feet, six inches tall; had brown hair and blue eyes; and weighed around 110 pounds. His coat had a tag reading "H.M. Lindenthal, Chicago." His shirt bore the laundry mark "Jones." His pocket watch had the initials "W.A." on the outside and "L.H.D." on the inner case. Evidently, he looked neater than the average hobo, as coroner Ernest Ashurst thought he appeared to be "well-bred" and from "an excellent family."

Anxious telegrams and phone calls inundated the coroner. A number of people from central Kentucky and as far away as Cincinnati came to McMeekin and Ashurst Funeral Home, thinking the boy might be a missing relative. All went away disappointed. Despite the widely disseminated description and the clues on his person, the police did not discover the traveler's identity. Citizens laid him to rest at community expense at Georgetown Cemetery on April 14. Coroner Ashurst said that he embalmed the youth so well that his remains should be identifiable for the next twenty years, should any possible relatives turn up. The sad, poetic inscription Georgetown residents carved on his tombstone memorialized their sympathy for the pleasant-looking stranger: "Some Mother's Boy."

His identity was the subject of speculation for decades. He certainly was not a local. Did he come from another region of Kentucky? Or from another state? Why did his family not come forward despite all of the publicity? Were they unaware of his death or did they just not care? Did they miss him or wonder where he had gone?

The unknown boy slept through a global economic depression; a second world war; the development of the atom bomb; decades of political unrest and changing social mores; a few additional wars; and developments in technology that would have seemed like wild-eyed science fiction had he heard about them on his last day on earth in the spring of '21. One of those technological developments would settle the question of his identity nearly a century after his death.

The Scott County coroner in 2016, John Goble, had a longstanding interest in the local enigma. He researched missing persons of the era and found that nineteen-year-old Frank Haynes of Bronston, Pulaski County, had run away from home in a fit of anger after his father had accused him of theft just a few days before Some Mother's Boy was killed in Georgetown. Haynes's family and friends neither saw nor heard from him again. Goble thought the timing interesting and found two women in Pulaski County who were nieces of the missing Haynes—relatives who could provide DNA samples to compare to Some Mother Boy's DNA.

On March 20, 2017, Georgetown officials and the National Missing and Unidentified Persons System (NAMUS) opened the grave. There wasn't much left, just a few bones and teeth, but the remains provided sufficient DNA. One of the Pulaski

County women provided a blood sample, and in June, science confirmed that Some Mother's Boy was Frank Haynes.

Strangely, the mystery never was a mystery among Haynes's immediate family, who knew all along that he was buried in the pauper's grave in Georgetown Cemetery. "According to officials with NAMUS," said a story posted at news station WLEX's website, "Haynes's father had seen photos of the dead boy and attempted to identify him, but had insufficient evidence to prove that the young man was his son."

Well-wishers exhumed Haynes and reburied him with his family at Newell Cemetery in Bronston. His new tombstone reads, "Frank Albert Haynes. Mar. 2, 1902—Apr. 1, 1921. Returned home June 26, 2017."

PEARL'S HEAD

The murder of Pearl Bryan is still so renowned—still the subject of so many books, articles and web pages—that only a summary is necessary before offering my two cents' worth. Readers who crave more details certainly will have no difficulty finding them.

Bryan was an attractive young blonde living in late nineteenth-century Greencastle, Indiana, when a cad and ne'er-do-well from Maine, Scott Jackson, seduced her. When Pearl became pregnant in the autumn of 1895, Jackson ditched her and enrolled in a Cincinnati dental college to escape the consequences of his actions. Pearl followed him there on January 28, 1896, insisting that he marry her. He, on the other hand, pressured her to have an abortion, to which she reluctantly agreed.

Jackson enlisted help from his equally nefarious but far less clever dental school roommate, Alonzo Walling. The two gave Pearl a veritable pharmacopeia of drugs intended to induce a spontaneous abortion, to no avail. On January 31, unable to afford a professional abortionist, Jackson and Walling desperately played the last miserable card in their hand: after drugging Pearl to near insensibility with cocaine, they took her across the river to Kentucky. They stabbed Pearl on the Fort Thomas farm of John B. Locke and callously dumped her nearly fully clothed body out in the open. A terrified teenage passerby found the corpse the next morning.

The murder of Pearl Bryan might have been forgotten except for one shocking, immortalizing detail: Pearl was not only stabbed, she was decapitated while alive, and her killers took the head away. No one ever found it, at least not officially. Despite recent foolish, sensational talk about Jackson and Walling beheading Pearl because they were in a Satanic cult (in 1896 Cincinnati?), it seems clear that they believed that it would make the body impossible to identify.

No doubt Jackson and Walling congratulated themselves on committing what they believed to be a perfect murder. Their smugness was short-lived: within days, a merchant back home in Greencastle positively identified the body by its distinctive shoes. Jackson was captured because of a damning letter he foolishly wrote to a friend in Indiana who happened to be Pearl's cousin. Jackson, the man who had betrayed Pearl, had a motive in seeing her out of the picture. When arrested, he incriminated his roommate. Whether Jackson or Walling, or both, committed the murder will remain unknown until the Endtime—neither confessed and each blamed the other. They were hanged at Newport on March 20, 1897.

That was the end of the murderers, but what became of Pearl's head? The major theory proposed at the time was that the killers carried it from the murder scene in her own alligator-hide valise, which is now in the collection of the Campbell County Historical and Genealogical Society. On January 31, the night of the murder, Jackson left the valise with a Cincinnati bartender named Legner, asking him to hold onto it until further notice. And, added Jackson, don't let anyone have it but me! Legner noticed that something inside the bag rolled around, not unlike a bowling ball. However, he was true to his promise and didn't take a peep.

The next night, February 1, Jackson returned for the valise and left the saloon. He came back fifteen minutes later and again asked Legner to watch the small suitcase for him. Legner noticed that the valise was lighter now, without the rolling object that had been inside. Had Jackson and Walling carried the valise to their dental school, where they burned the head in a furnace or perhaps tossed it in a sewer?

This time, Jackson did not return for his property. After Jackson's arrest, Legner finally got suspicious and informed the authorities about the valise. An inspection revealed blond hairs and blood smears inside it.

That would seem to solve the puzzle of what the killers did with Pearl's head. However, though they were breathtakingly incompetent, it strains credulity that they would bring a valise containing a human head to a public saloon and *leave it there* for an entire day, especially when the rest of Pearl's body was waiting to be discovered. What if Legner had curiously peeked inside? Why didn't Jackson just carry it straight to the dental college on January 31, before the body was found, and throw the bundle in the furnace, valise and all? In addition, there are practical problems with the furnace cremation theory. It requires the hellish heat of a crematorium to destroy a human body; an ordinary school furnace won't get the job done. A skull in particular is difficult to burn since it is large and consists of thick bones. Teeth are incredibly durable. If police inspected the dental school furnace in 1896—and they probably did, since that was the favored solution to the mystery of Pearl's missing head even then—some remains should have been found. Even in a crematorium, bone fragments survive the fire.

While the head in the valise might be the best solution to the mystery, a few forgotten incidents offer other possibilities. On November 15, 1900, George Girty was picking wholesome walnuts on John B. Locke's farm when he found a very unwholesome object: a weather-beaten skull in privet bushes, "a stone's throw" from where Pearl Bryan's body had been found. As it turned out, a fellow named John Darnell had found the head first, two weeks previously—but instead of informing the police, he took two of its teeth as souvenirs and stuck the skull on a tree, where it patiently awaited its chance to frighten Girty.

Sheriff Plummer examined the cranium and said that it closely matched descriptions of Pearl's physiognomy. The skull was small, suggesting it was a woman's. It still had a tooth with a gold filling, as did the two teeth filched by the incurious Darnell. Pearl Bryan's Greencastle dentist, Dr. Gillespie, confirmed that she had gold fillings.

All in all a very interesting find, especially considering its location, but the skull was never confirmed as Pearl's, and its present whereabouts, if any, are unknown. One can't help wondering if Jackson and Walling would have been so stupid as to superficially dispose of their victim's noggin so close to her body when, with just a little more effort, they could have buried it, tossed it in the river, burned it and so on. But then, they *were* quite incompetent murderers.

On February 17, 1907, C.G. Glandorf, a Cincinnati contractor, was filling in a piece of ground between Newport and Dayton, Kentucky, when a laborer found a second buried skull. (Strange to relate, Glandorf lived only a street away from the boardinghouse where Jackson and Walling had roomed as students.) Anatomists declared the skull a young woman's. A soil sample analysis determined that the dirt that had covered the cranium formed part of the roadway Jackson and Walling would have taken from Newport to Fort Thomas after crossing the Ohio River from Cincinnati.

Also, the skull's measurements matched Pearl's head. No word as to whether it had gold fillings, however.

If only investigators had preserved the skull, we might now do DNA tests to determine whether it was Pearl's. However, on March 8, they did what was then considered the respectable thing: they burned it as best they could in the basement furnace of the Newport City Building. A reporter noted that the ceremony was "not very solemn." The head was ruined, and so was probably the last chance of solving the mystery forever, unless someone on a camping trip just happens to unearth an old female skull that science can identify as Pearl's.

As a final observation, in both the 1900 and 1907 incidents, *only* a skull was found—not an entire skeleton, as one would expect. So either of these crania could have been Pearl's. Or maybe both of them!

CIRCUS TROUBLE

The circus! Clowns, popcorn, equestrians and elephants! Also, sometimes, destruction, accidents and crime rampant and variegated!

The residents of Garrard County got the thrills of the carnival and the excitement of a train wreck combined when several cars of a Sells Brothers circus locomotive fell off the track near Moran Summit on the morning of September 24, 1882. Early rumors held that fifteen men died, sixty were wounded and that all the wild animals escaped and were on the prowl for Garrard Countians to eat.

In sober reality, fifteen cars out of twenty-one toppled over a fifteen-foot embankment. Eleven passengers had minor injuries, two had fatal wounds and three died instantly. Two of the dead were attachés of the circus, and one was Willis Underwood, an eighteen-year-old from Mount Vernon, Kentucky, who was stealing a ride. A tiger—merely one, but fear multiplied him—escaped its cage. Bystanders were terrified as the beast walked about and licked its chops. However, the denouement couldn't have been gentler and more unexpected: as the sun rose, the tiger walked back into the cage on its own volition. The Sells Brothers lost much property, including figures used in historical tableaux and its electric light. The train's engine was unharmed and went to Lancaster to retrieve "surgeons and coffins."

A coroner's inquest next day determined that the accident was due to negligence by both the railroad and the circus people. The train had only four working brakes and thus came downhill too quickly; in fact, the circus folks *intentionally* had removed some brakes to make loading wagons on the

cars easier. Engineer Jack Foley swore that he was traveling only thirty miles an hour, but witnesses estimated that he was going twice that. The two circus men killed in the wreck, Ben Case and Jack Carter, were buried near Paint Lick, far from home and family.

The wreck cost the railroad $10,000, and Sells Brothers also faced financial punishment: it had to cancel an engagement in London, Laurel County, which it expected to be extra lucrative because it would have been its first performance there.

Unbelievably, engineer Foley had another wreck the next day in almost the same spot. As he headed from Paint Lick to Silver Creek, he ran into another train at Moran Summit and demolished his own engine. No one was injured, but bystanders heard the engineer remark that he was "going to leave that ill-fated country."

ALMOST ONE MONTH LATER, Kentucky was the scene of a second circus train wreck. On October 23, 1882, Adam Forepaugh's Circus crashed on the C&O railroad tracks near West Point, Hardin County. As in the former crash, cars went over an embankment. There were no fatalities, but as a newspaper remarked, "Had the train been moving at its usual rapidity the wild animals would have been scattered all over the country." The show made it to Louisville the next day. The *Courier-Journal* praised the show for having "many features of excellence which made a first-class ring exhibition" but could not resist complaining that "the jokes of the clowns [were] very bad, even for circus jokes." But it must be hard for even clowns to achieve boffo laffs after experiencing a train wreck.

ON AUGUST 16, 1889, three pretty blond teenage girls from Evansville, Indiana, ventured to Henderson, Kentucky, and eagerly waited at the levee for the arrival of a steamer carrying Orton's Circus and Wild West Combination. The reason for their anxiety became as plain as the bulbous, candy-colored nose on a clown's face when the ship arrived: the girls had run away from home and were waiting for their secret lovers, described uncharitably by an Owensboro newspaper as "three ugly clowns." The girls went so far as to rent rooms in a boardinghouse, presumably so they could indulge in a three-ring orgy combining the joys of illicit loving with pie tossing. This presumption is strengthened by the fact that one of the randy clowns took the precaution of going to the courthouse first on the pretense of getting a false marriage license just in case any nosey persons asked questions. Police officers caught wind of the scheme, went to the boardinghouse and ordered the girls to return clownlessly (look, I coined a word!) to Evansville. The crestfallen teens obeyed and returned to their folks, who undoubtedly thought up creative punishments for disgracing themselves and their families by running off—with *clowns*.

"It is to be hoped," moralized the *Henderson Journal*, "they will forget the allurements of paint, tights, and spangles."

FOLLOWING THE GREAT SUCCESS of Buffalo Bill Cody's Wild West Show, similarly western-themed traveling circuses inundated the eastern states. One was Buckskin Bill's Wild West Show, formed in 1900. The name was shamelessly misleading, as it originated not out west but in Paducah. Perhaps its founders, brothers Ed and Fletcher Terrell, figured far western *Kentucky* was close enough. The flimflam didn't end there. While Cody was definitely a historical personage, there was no real Buckskin Bill. The Terrells hired an actor to portray the fictitious frontiersman.

If BBWWS was famous for anything, it was the mayhem and criminality that followed everywhere in its wake. On August 3, 1900, when the showmen were setting up at Marion, Crittenden County, a few local youths came to watch, one of whom was a black man named Pickens. The circus men clubbed the spectators for reasons not supplied and sent them packing. At midnight, Claude C. Wheeler, an outraged member of "one of the oldest and wealthiest families of the county," armed himself and went to the depot to investigate. While the Buckskin Bill folks were unloading their wagons, Wheeler demanded to know if the youths' allegation was true. A number of cowboys knocked Wheeler down, and the injured man crawled under a wagon. The showmen dragged him into the open, fired twenty shots at him and pounded him on the head with a club—the old *argumentum ad cranium*. A bystander hurried away, and when help arrived, Wheeler had three mortal gunshot wounds and two skull fractures. The assailants also stole his pistol and watch, so it doesn't sound much like a case of self-defense.

The show quickly pulled up stakes and went to Caldwell County, where the sheriff arrested four members at Princeton on August 4. One was a thirteen-year-old orphan named Jim Terrell, almost certainly a relative of the show's founders. The three adults were taken to Marion and then hustled right back to Princeton after a mob threatened to lynch them, western-style.

The legal authorities of Crittenden County wasted no time. The three adult cowboys went on trial on August 10, although they dropped charges against young Terrell. The trial "attract[ed] the largest crowds ever seen here," said a newspaper correspondent, which the showmen must have found gratifying. The defense argued that the sheriff arrested the wrong men, and in any case, Wheeler had been intoxicated and started the fight. There was confusion among eyewitnesses as to whether Wheeler or the showmen fired first, and testimony tended to show that the defendants were not present, at least not when the shooting began. The jury acquitted them on August 11. Nevertheless, *some* members of the show used excessive force against Wheeler, and they got lucky twice. The violent episode began, as noted, when the circus men clubbed a few young men, including one named Pickens. In the third week of September, Pickens died of his injuries. But by then the show was far away.

On June 5, 1902, Buckskin Bill's roustabouts were erecting a tent at Cynthiana when the show's press agent, John Leehy, got into an argument with a laborer. When Leehy turned his back, the worker knocked him unconscious with a tent peg and ran away. This sort of head injury never seems to do anything worse to the Three Stooges than provide an amusing sound effect not unlike two coconuts colliding, but in the real world, Leehy's injury was fatal. The show's cowboys and Indians tracked the roustabout over Harrison County's lovely countryside, but he made his escape.

In a bizarre coincidence, on the very same day, an identical assault took place at a different traveling show in Kentucky. Reed's Trained Animal Show was setting up at Owingsville, Bath County, when one worker fatally injured another by striking him in the head with a tent stake. Friendly warning: Tent pegs make handy weapons for surly show folk.

Buckskin Bill's employees were simply unable to keep out of trouble, and their most serious breach of the law occurred on June 17, 1902, a few days after the tent stake murder. While attending a show at Vanceburg, Lewis County, sixteen-year-old Laura Belle M., daughter of a prominent farmer at Ruggles, was separated from her parents. Laura Belle was described by the press as "beautiful" but "half-witted," making her, as a *Courier-Journal* headline said, "an easy victim of showmen's wiles." Buckskin Bill's opportunistic ruffians were exactly in the mood for a pretty but mentally challenged underage girl. They coaxed her into one of the show train's boxcars and held her prisoner. The train stayed in Vanceburg for the night, and they spent that time "repeatedly assaulting" Laura Belle as her frantic parents searched for her.

Next morning at Garrison, a few miles from Vanceburg, the Buckskin Bill men literally threw Laura Belle off the train, fearing that they were about to be caught. Fortunately, a trainman saw her eviction and rescued her. "She was not much hurt by the fall," said a news account, "but was nearly dead from the horrible treatment."

Police arrested four of the circus men at Ashland, Boyd County, on June 18, just as they were putting on their cowboy and Indian costumes. Laura Belle identified three of them, although the law suspected more were guilty. The authorities sent the trio she named to Vanceburg, where they were threatened by the to-be-expected mob. (The fourth man, whose guilt was debatable, was held at Catlettsburg as a material witness.) The three cast further doubt on their innocence when they tried to break out of jail. They nearly succeeded and as punishment had to wear handcuffs for the duration.

The incident with Laura Belle aside, the Buckskin Bill Show's behavior had been so bad in Vanceburg that they were denied permission ever to exhibit there again, "owing to the tough element that is either connected with it or following it," according to a press account, which further noted that a number of robberies had occurred while they were in town. They were unwelcome even in their hometown, as made clear by the *Paducah News-Democrat*: "If it's all the same to Col. Buckskin Bill, Paducah would rather he located his next winter's quarters somewhere else."

One of Laura Belle's captors, William P., had an examining trial on June 21; police released the other two for lack of evidence. Testimony from witnesses showed that Laura Belle was a perfect victim: she had never been to school and was so unsophisticated that Vanceburg and Martinsburg were the only cities she had ever seen. In fact, when she went to the Buckskin Bill performance, it was the first time she had been in Vanceburg, and it was the first show of *any* sort that she had attended. She was so naïve and green that she would talk to any stranger. When she got to the Wild West show, she thought William P. was sorta cute and told him she was interested in joining the circus. That was all the opening he needed to trick her into getting in that train car.

Nevertheless, the evidence against William was not as strong as the prosecution wished. No one saw him lead or force the girl into the boxcar; the trainman who saw men kicking Laura Belle off the moving train did not see William doing it. Another railroad man said that William had confessed to abducting Laura Belle, and his unsupported claim was the best evidence. In September, the grand jury failed to return an indictment against him, and presumably, he rejoined his fellow lowlifes at Buckskin Bill's Wild West Show, where bad behavior seemed to be in the job description. According to the Western Trips website, "[S]ome members of Buckskin Bill's were accused of other murders, arson and kidnapping. One spectator was shot and killed accidentally during one performance. There was also an instance of several employees fil[ing] suit on Fletcher Terrell when he didn't pay them....The show had trouble from the start and seemed to be cursed."

Eventually, two genuine (though retired) elderly outlaws toured with the show: Cole Younger and Jesse James's brother Frank. In 1903, James and Younger split from the Buckskin Bill organization and formed their own Wild West show. Legend holds that Younger persuaded a manager to release him from his contract by pulling a gun on him, an argument that the executive found far more convincing than mere words.

SOMETIMES TRAVELING CIRCUSES PREYED on their own employees instead of the locals. On October 24, 1914, Kit Carson's Buffalo Ranch Wild West Show appeared at Barbourville, Knox County. It was its final show, and the workers' payday had come, including back wages. Even so, because the show was in financial arrears, the laborers were told that they'd have to be satisfied with slashed wages; so if a performer were owed $110, for example, he or she would have to settle for $40. However, they didn't even get that much. The manager fled in the night, stranding the entire company, including members who had no train fare home. The *Barbourville Democrat* shed an editorial tear over their plight:

> *We have seen many cases of distress but this beats all. Men who had worked for seven long weeks and had not taken up any wages, in the hope of having money to pay their way home at least, were turned away by these cold-blooded managers with a very small pittance and sometimes without anything. Many women among them were running about wild with excitement because they were left stranded in a strange land, most of them weeping. More than a hundred colored men were turned loose without one cent, poorly clad; in fact, many of them barefooted. A warrant was sworn out for the manager, but he made his escape, and these people are left to weed their row in a strange land with times hard and positions hard to find.*

A CIRCUS CAME TO Olive Hill, Carter County, on April 26, 1915. The audience got an unexpected thrill for their shiny new nickels when Frank White, the lion tamer, encountered a big cat that refused to go along with the act. When other performers removed White from the cage, he was a head shorter than when he entered.

FEMALE CIRCUS PERFORMERS AT Paris, Bourbon County, were annoyed on the night of August 2, 1916, when they realized that a Peeping Tom was getting a free eyeful of their pulchritude through the folds of their dressing tent. Enraged employees caught him after a chase and gave him a vigorous beating that one would not normally associate with the entertainment industry. They were going to lynch him too, but a police officer rescued him at the last minute.

CONSIDERING THE MANY DEPREDATIONS committed by old-time traveling circuses in Kentucky, it seems only fair to end with an account of a battle royale between mountain bullies and carnival men in which the latter were the victims rather than instigators. Hunting and Hilliard's Great Pacific Circus had an exhibition at Red Lick, on the Jackson–Madison County border, on April 23, 1878. A crowd of moonshine-swilling toughs, headed by one Jeff Benge, attacked them, determined to break up the act and force the show on its way. The circus men fought back with pistols and those seemingly omnipresent tent pegs, killing a roughneck named James Baker and wounding three others. Said an entertainment-loving newspaper correspondent who clearly sided with the circus: "The only regret is that the list of killed amongst the bullies was not larger. None of the showmen were hurt."

DON'T GET BACK TO WHERE YOU ONCE BELONGED, JO-JO

Treat the biographies of circus freaks of times past with caution; like Hollywood studio press releases of a later era, the proprietors of the shows had a stake in making the performers seem as exotic as possible. Thus, their "official" life stories teem with exaggerations, unsupportable claims and outright fabrication. Historians should be skeptical when researching the history of that hair-covered wonder of the sideshow, Jo-Jo the Dog-Faced Boy.

Legendary showman P.T. Barnum brought the teenage Jo-Jo to America in 1884. Barnum, the purveyor of the Fiji Mermaid hoax (and sundry others), concocted a yarn about his new prize attraction's having lived with his similarly hirsute father in the wilds of Kostroma, Russia, before being caught by trappers.

Calmer minds declared that the young man actually was born in St. Petersburg in 1868, was perfectly civilized and that his name was Fedor Jeftichew. Everyone agreed, however, that he looked remarkably like a dog—the breed to which he was most commonly compared was the Skye terrier—and that he owed his appearance to a rare disease called hypertrichosis, which results in a luxurious growth of hair all over the body. Hypertrichosis is hereditary, and it appears that Jo-Jo's father made his living as a circus attraction known throughout Europe as the Man-Dog.

Jo-Jo's act consisted of contradictions. Barnum had the idea of dressing the young man like a Russian cavalry officer, creating a juxtaposition between the primitive wildness of his face and the elegance of his clothes; the most famous photos of Jo-Jo feature him in this costume of blue velvet coat and large brass buttons. His appearance also contrasted with his clearly good-natured personality. Barnum coached him to bark, growl and snap at audiences, but they could tell it was all an act and he played his "ferociousness" for laughs. Despite his brute-like countenance, he was highly intelligent and could speak German, Russian and French. (Later he also learned English.)

So, what has this to do with Kentucky? Jo-Jo toured the Bluegrass State at least twice. He made an appearance near the beginning of his long career at Louisville's Liederkranz Hall on November 11, 1886. Crowds turned out to see him despite bad weather. For the price of admittance, they also gawked at the Transparent Turk and a strange being billed as Silva the Half-Woman. (To this writer's unmitigated glee, the *Courier-Journal* carried news about Jo-Jo and his fellow freaks in the same column with news about a performance of the opera *Faust* and the ritzy coming-out party of debutante Annie Bell Bijur. She was "not only one of the most beautiful of Kentucky's far-famed daughters, but also a young lady of much brightness and of charming personality.")

Jo-Jo's other documented trip to Kentucky came in April 1887, when he visited Richmond in Madison County—admission fifty cents a head, half-price for children under nine years of age! By then, he was working for Barrett's Circus rather than for Barnum. It consisted of three rings, complete with vaudeville acts, gladiatorial feats, acrobats, Japanese jugglers, tightrope walkers, wrestlers, swordsmen, a racetrack, hee-larious though nightmare-inducing clowns and a re-creation of life in the Wild West. The traveling circus also featured a menagerie, including elephants, camels, giraffes, a two-horned rhino, gazelles, zebras, a lion, a black Japanese tiger, a Bengal tiger and a hippopotamus. Nevertheless, Jo-Jo clearly was the star of the show: his canine countenance dominated the newspaper ad. He was deemed "undoubtedly the most wonderful and inexplicable human phenomenon that this age has ever seen." Let us hope such extravagant praise didn't go to his hairy head. If it did, perhaps a line in the advertisement brought him back down to earth: "No extra charge to see Jo-Jo."

The show played in Richmond on April 29. The next week's local paper, the *Kentucky Register*, had compliments for the wild animals and displayed freaks, including a Turkish giant called Colonel Goshen, a dwarf, a tattooed man and "frizzled-head girls." However, the editor called Jo-Jo "the great attraction" and for some reason seemed especially impressed that he smoked cigarettes. Sadly for posterity, Jo-Jo's thoughts on Richmond are unrecorded. When the circus left town for Winchester, it undoubtedly left in its wake scores of little boys who wished they also were dog-faced.

(Here's a nugget of obscure information that did not fit in any of my other books and barely fits here at that: Madison County can claim its very own once-esteemed, though now forgotten, circus freak. William Vaughn of Big Hill on the Jackson County border was the Living Skeleton for the Barnum & Bailey and John Robinson Circuses for years. Reportedly, he was out of showbiz by the end of March 1895 when his father, John Vaughn, died at

age 104, "probably the oldest man in Kentucky," as though the family had not already attained sufficient glory. The erstwhile Living Skeleton died of pneumonia at age sixty-five at Long Branch on October 28, 1906. At the time of his death, Vaughn was six feet, six inches tall and weighed less than fifty pounds. He is buried at Richmond Cemetery.)

Jo-Jo kept wowing (or bow-wowing?) audiences with his doggishness until he died of pneumonia in Greece on January 31, 1904. Unlike most human oddities who are famous for a while and then pass into oblivion, like poor William Vaughn, Jo-Jo was not forgotten. References to him turn up surprisingly often in pop culture. To name just a few, episodes of *Star Trek* ("This Side of Paradise") and *The X-Files* ("Humbug") mention him. Former Mouseketeer Annette Funicello released a song in 1959 called "Jo-Jo the Dog-Faced Boy," in which our hairy hero rocks the kids out at a high school sock hop. And punk-pop rocker extraordinaire Joe King (aka Joe Queer) has been known to refer to himself as Joe-Joe the Dog-Faced Punk.

CLAY COUNTY CREEPINESS

TB Sheets

Visitors to the Wilson Cemetery at Burning Springs, close to the border of Clay and Jackson Counties, will notice a long, long line of grave markers for members of the Samuel Shepherd family. The death dates are remarkably close together for such a large family. Thereby hangs a tale told to me by Mildred Wilson McQueen that may be fact, legend or a blend of both. However, the smart money is on its being true.

The story goes that son Roy Shepherd died of tuberculosis on June 26, 1922, aged only four months. Then daughter Clarinda died of the same disease on July 24, 1925, at age nineteen. Son Ramey died of TB at age four years on April 15, 1928. Exactly a year later, another son, Reo, died of tuberculosis at age sixteen on April 15, 1929. The matriarch of the family, Louallie Shepherd, died of TB on August 22, 1931, aged forty-five. Death took a holiday for a while, but then son Ploy died of TB on February 1, 1940, just a few weeks short of his eighteenth birthday. Nearly a year later, his brother Elmer died of TB on February 22, 1941, at age twenty-four. The family patriarch, Samuel, died of TB on August 4, 1943, at age fifty-nine. Finally, sister Ruby, a high school student, died of TB on April 9, 1947, at age nineteen.

The contagious disease then called the white plague, the white death, phthisis or consumption more or less wiped out the entire family. The only survivors were brothers Oscar, who died in 1966 at age sixty-one, and Zelmer, who died in 1970 at age fifty.

Are the details of the ghastly story verifiable? Unfortunately, Clay County appears not to have kept death certificates consistently. Only Elmer and Ruby Shepherd have such records filed with the state, but these documents confirm that both died of pulmonary tuberculosis. It is said that after a certain point, the health authorities decided to burn down the Shepherd house, furniture and all, rather than risk allowing anyone else to live there.

HAMP TAKES FLIGHT

When Hamp Biggs was a young man, he rode a sled down a steep Clay County hill—some say it overlooked the Oneida Institute campus, others say it was Sandlin Hill—and as he zipped down the rocky terrain, he went through a fence and struck the roof of a small "tater shed," causing him to take flight. To the amazement of onlookers, Hamp survived the crash. The slang phrase "as dangerous as Hamp's sled" took on local currency.

When Biggs died on May 21, 1976, at age seventy-three, his son, Tim, created a unique square headstone with a hole in the center, seemingly made from a chimney flue and the capstone from a well. It bears the words commemorating Hamp's claim to fame: "As dangerous as Hamp's sled."

A SELF-MADE WIDOW

Fifty-year-old William Jones and his wife, Nellie, lived in a cabin on Otter Creek near the Knox County border. One day in January 1931, William just "up and disappeared," right after which the family cabin burned down. A neighbor, Dill Freeman, told everyone that William had gone to Harlan County to look for work.

A few months later, William's son, Mitchell, went searching for him. He found it hard to believe that his dad would just go away without telling him first. In addition, when Mitchell looked for his mother, Nellie, she was at Dill Freeman's house and appeared to have taken up residence.

Mitchell demanded his mother tell him just what had been going on. Nothing much, Nellie told him—only that Dill Freeman had decapitated a sleeping William with a single axe blow, set the house on fire and then made up the story about William going to Harlan County to distract everyone. Oh, and also, the reason I'm living with him is that he kidnapped me!

No, Mitchell didn't believe it either, and the same day he had murder warrants sworn out against his mother and Dill Freeman. On April 5, two deputy sheriffs and the town marshal went to Otter Creek to make some arrests. Easier said than done, as it required a twenty-mile trip on horseback into some of Clay County's wildest mountain scenery.

After the officers arrested the couple and took them to jail at Manchester, investigators learned that someone had removed valuables, including a shotgun, from William Jones's cabin before it had been set aflame. Dill Freeman's house contained these items. Dill had constructed a new cabin with haste on the site of the burned one, and when authorities scraped under it, they found human bones. Suddenly Dill Freeman and Nellie Jones were at cross-purposes. She stuck to her less-than-convincing tale of dastardly murder, arson and abduction, but Dill said that Nellie chopped off her husband's head. Not only that, he still had the axe—that's the sort of thing that makes a real keepsake.

The grand jury returned indictments against the couple on April 22. Then they *really* turned on each other. Nellie confessed to the Commonwealth's attorney that she had decapitated her husband while Dill Freeman stood watch with a shotgun and said that she would plead guilty in exchange for a life term. The attorney refused her offer and vowed to seek the death penalty for both.

Nellie's remorse was palpable and pathetic when the trial began on April 30. She admitted that she had struck her sleeping husband three times with an axe and told the jury, "I don't care what you do with me." Nellie and Dill were so foolish as to have committed their crimes with a witness nearby: William H., a teenage boarder at Dill's house, who heard the three chops.

On May 4, a jury voted for a death sentence for Dill and a life sentence for Nellie. Considering they were equally guilty, it is safe to assume that Nellie got a lighter sentence because she was a woman and for no better reason. Dill worried about having a very interesting experience in a very interesting chair at the state prison.

However, Dill's concern was unnecessary. On his last day in office, December 7, 1931, the outgoing Governor Sampson pardoned or commuted the sentences of 339 convicts in the Kentucky prison system. With the stroke of a pen, as though by magic, Dill's death sentence became life imprisonment.

One of the other persons whose sentence Sampson commuted was a Paducah woman who, back in 1923, had dynamited a pregnant woman whom she considered a romantic rival, along with the victim's three children. Sampson freed her on the condition that she move out of Kentucky and never come back, thereby making her some other state's potential problem. Perhaps one could argue that the governor was a *bit* softhearted.

FEUD FOR THOUGHT

Clay County was once such a violent place that in February 1933, the Kentucky legislature considered abolishing it to end "clan contests [feuds, that is] which have made the county notorious for nearly half a century," as State Inspector and Examiner Nat Sewell put it. Sewell explained further: "In no other county in the state has lawlessness prevailed for so long a time with such disastrous results to the people, nor has the character of crime reached the barbaric level in any other part of the state that has been in evidence in recent years in Clay."

The plan to break up Clay County by merging it with surrounding counties was never carried out and gradually forgotten, but why would legislators consider such drastic measures in the first place? The following story may give some idea.

On June 18, 1935, someone shot James Cupp to death in a section of Clay that the county's circuit judge described as being especially rife with "shootings, burnings, and carrying of high-powered guns and pistols." No one dared reveal to the press the name of Cupp's assassin, but those in the know said he was "a good friend" of the victim. As of the next day, police had not issued a warrant for this man's arrest.

Pallbearers carried Cupp's casket to the family graveyard on June 19. Once there, shots rang out from three sections of underbrush. The mourners cast aside all notions of social decorum befitting the solemn occasion and lammed it on foot back to the house of Cupp's mother. (The record does not state whether they carried the coffin with them as they ran or abandoned it in the cemetery; if the former, that must really have been something to see.) When they regained their nerve, they vowed they would bury Cupp the next day.

Meanwhile, the press tells us, the still publicly unnamed man who had killed Cupp was strutting about with impunity. However, he must have been worried that some plot against his life was afoot, as he went "armed and accompanied by fifteen or twenty armed men."

On June 24, Cupp's assassin made the critical error of going for a walk without his squadron of bodyguards. A mob hiding in the bushes ambushed him as he strolled down a road near his house, no doubt while he felt secure and was contemplating all the funny little mysteries of life. Now that he was safely dead, authorities and the press revealed that he was Earl Porter, "the third man within a week to die 'with his boots on' in this county." (The second man was Bobbie Baker, shot to death just like his father, grandfather, brother and nephew. It was kind of a family tradition.)

A warrant finally had been issued for Earl's arrest before his untimely end, but it seemed rather beside the point now.

THE GREAT MADISON COUNTY MONKEY HOAX

I have written before of Joseph Mulhattan, the traveling hardware salesman who lived in Louisville in the 1880s and '90s and who became world-famous for the wild tall tales he wrote in convincingly deadpan style and sent to newspapers while on his travels. For a time, Mulhattan, using the pen name "Orange Blossom," was as much a household name as Mark Twain. One of his most notorious hoaxes originated in Madison County, Kentucky.

According to a contemporary account, early in February 1887, Mulhattan heard a yarn about a Texas cotton farmer who employed trained apes as laborers; if true, Mulhattan probably read the original story in the *Victoria (TX) Advocate*. However, in a 1904 interview, he claimed to have gotten his inspiration from showman P.T. Barnum's trained elephants.

While staying in Richmond, Mulhattan rewrote the tale but gave it his own twist and his trademark dose of realism. He claimed that the unorthodox solution to the labor problem was factual, and he credited the experiment to his friend James B. Parkes. Mulhattan telegraphed his tale to the *Louisville Courier-Journal*. The story was prominently headlined "A Monkey Story" in the February 17, 1887 issue:

> RICHMOND, *Feb. 16.—Mr. J.B. Parkes, a substantial farmer near Kingston…has successfully trained a force of seven large monkeys to work in his hemp fields, and to break and prepare the hemp for market. They do the work quicker and better than the Negroes he employed, and the cost is about one-fourth. It required about four months of patient training to get the*

*animals to fully understand the duties required of them. But now they seem
to comprehend it all and perform their daily labor with but little difficulty.
The monkeys were sent to Mr. Parkes by his brother, who is engaged in
business in Cape Town, South Africa, and who had seen the animals put to
similar uses by the natives of that country. Mr. Parkes will send for about
ten more, six of which will be sold to John G. Taylor, another extensive
raiser of hemp and neighbor of Mr. Parkes.*

Aside from the uncomfortable joke concerning the apes being better laborers than black workers, the hoax is so convincingly worded that even today it might fool the casual browser. The *Courier-Journal* was wary of the tale and correctly guessed its origin. The front page of the February 17 edition briefly summarized the story of the seven laboring monkeys before delivering a genial insult: "[W]e desire to say that this office does not know if Mr. Mulhattan is in Madison County or not, but there is a suspicion that he is; in point of fact, there may be seven of him there." The next day, the paper joked that the monkeys were probably saving up to buy some hand organs.

The *Courier-Journal* may have been skeptical, but other papers and many of their readers readily believed the hoax, as it contains a trace of social commentary under the surface. In February 1887, the nation faced a crisis due to a series of labor strikes. As one newspaper remarked, "The present year is but a little over forty days old, yet there has [*sic*] been over one hundred strikes of workingmen during that time, or an average of nearly three for every working day." Like the best urban legends, Mulhattan's hoax had an implied moral: *Don't go on strike, because a trained monkey could replace you!* Perhaps the fake news story was so effective because it "confirmed" our hidden fear that any laborer is expendable.

Newspapers from coast to coast reprinted the hoax. A correspondent in Shelby County, Kentucky, got in on the act by insisting to the *Courier-Journal* that he personally knew that James B. Parkes's brother-in-law, James V. Goodman, had a labor force of four monkeys. On February 17, the *Louisville Times* featured an editorial on the subject of "this latest conspiracy against the rights of labor." It is difficult to assess the tone of the piece, but judging from the writer's earnestness, it seems he believed every word of it:

> [Madison County] *is the home of Senator Harris, one of the leading candidates for Governor, and* [the monkey story] *may raise an issue which will play a very important part in deciding the gubernatorial contest. It is just this: Does Senator Harris indorse* [sic] *the course pursued by his neighbor? Is he in favor of monkey labor against man labor? If the free and independent workmen of Kentucky are to be displaced by imported monkeys, the men who are responsible for it should be known, that any claims they may make for public recognition be spurned by a justly indignant Commonwealth....*
>
> *If these monkeys can be taught to harvest hemp, why may not their instruction reach to planting and plowing corn, sowing and reaping wheat, hoeing and stripping tobacco; in fact, to all the manifold and arduous duties which give employment to such large numbers of men in agricultural pursuits. This is a shameless invasion of human rights which could only find its origin in that selfish and monopolistic spirit which seems to pervade all classes of society in these latter days. It should be discountenanced and repressed.*
>
> *Labor questions are the most delicate and difficult with which politicians have to deal....Is the question of monkey labor to be one of prime influence in this State? Senator Harris, in whose county this innovation had its origin, should speak out at once. Is he with the monkeys or with the men?*

The next day, the *Times*, possibly fearing it had been had, insisted that the monkey report was plausible. The editor quoted an authoritative passage from the journal *Science*: "M. Victor Meunier, a French physiologist...asks not only that the ape shall be made a domestic animal like the dog, but that it shall be properly trained in various domestic duties and even prepared by a regular course of instruction to take its place as a factory operative in our large industrial establishments. Such an employment of the manlike animals, thinks M. Meunier, 'would utilize in the service of humanity much cheap labor that is now allowed to waste.'"

The *Times*'s staff soon realized it indeed had been "sold," for the editorial page stiffly announced on February 19, "Over-credulous people are hereby warned against the *Courier-Journal*'s monkey correspondents in Madison and Shelby Counties. All those stories about the introduction of monkey labor into the hemp-fields are the weak inventions of weaker imitators of Joe Mulhattan." Those "over-credulous" people, of course, included the editorial staff of the *Times*. Even their correction was in error, for Mulhattan himself had created the original fake item.

The *New York Sun* ran an editorial on the subject on February 21. Like the *Louisville Times*, the *Sun* appeared to believe the story, which it found improbable but not impossible: "Whether this particular story be true or false, there is no doubt that the more docile and intelligent of apes have been instructed to perform work very much like that to which Mr. Parkes is said to have trained his seven monkeys after four months of patient tuition." The *Sun* proved its point with several examples drawn from the *Revue Scientifique* and other reliable sources but jokingly decried monkeys' lack of honesty.

Another paper that fell for the hoax was the *Houston Post*, which remarked editorially on February 26, "The Kentucky farmer who employs monkeys in his hemp fields has undoubtedly discovered the 'missing link.' Darwin died too soon." Meanwhile, the *Dayton Journal* predicted a war between the Knights of Labor and the "foreign pauper labor" represented by Parkes's monkeys.

Hemp-farming apes seemed to the *Chicago Tribune* a subject worthy of the poetic instinct:

> *The President scratched his puzzled head,*
> *And wearily to himself he said:*
> *"If I make Smith and Jones Commissioners,*
> *Why, I snub the Brown petitioners.*
> *Let me think. By all that's lucky!*
> *A ray of hope comes from Kentucky!*
> *....I'll bounce this army of bilks and flunkeys,*
> *And make my choice from the working monkeys."*

A contemporary newspaper reader could be forgiven for being confused by the clash between the assertions that the monkey story was a hoax and all the equally plausible counter-assertions, some by alleged eyewitnesses, that it was genuine. The story reached its apex of notoriety on February 17 when the nation's paper of record, the *New York Times*, mentioned it on page one, with the added information that furious labor organizations intended to boycott Parkes. In the same issue, the *Times* included an editorial (headlined "Scab Monkeys") concerning the disturbing primate labor situation in

Kentucky. The tone of the piece is tongue-in-cheek and shows that the *Times* did not fall for Mulhattan's hoax:

> *Loyal Knights of Labor should view with alarm and resist with clubs the movement to introduce imported monkey labor in this Republic. The movement, to be sure, is as yet in its beginning. Only one American citizen is thus far reported as an employer of monkeys. The man who has aimed this dastardly blow at organized labor is J.B. PARKES, of Kingston, Ky....If this thing is not stopped we shall presently have millions of pauper monkeys in this country, working merely for their board and lodgings and excluding an equal or greater number of Italians and Irishmen from gainful occupations. This must not be; the Simian must go....A delegation of Knights of Labor should proceed at once to Kingston, where they should hang those seven scab monkeys with their own hemp, put the miserable PARKES under the ban of a perpetual boycott, and send such a letter of warning to his collusive brother in South Africa as would cause him to abandon forthwith his abhorrent industry as a monkey purveyor.*

The *Courier-Journal*, amused by the mock-serious *New York Times* editorial, reprinted it twice within a week. In turn, newspapers across the country copied the editorial from either the *Times* or the *Courier-Journal*—and not always with the caveat that the piece was not serious. As an indication of what a sensation the monkey hoax created, the *Hopkinsville Semi-Weekly South Kentuckian* reprinted the *New York Times*'s editorial on page one almost a year after the hoax broke.

How many laborers and casual readers did not get the joke and believed that cheap and efficient ape labor had endangered their jobs? We can only guess, though apparently it was quite a few. According to historians Fred Allen Engle and Robert N. Grise, "For several weeks Parkes received about twenty-five letters a day, some berating him for putting 'honest, hardworking laborers out of work,' but most inquiring about the practicability of the experiment." Another indicator of public reaction is that black laborers from Shelby, Henry and Jefferson Counties met in Simpsonville on the night of February 26 to solemnly protest monkey labor, which they feared was a threat to their livelihoods. They unanimously adopted the following resolution:

> *WHEREAS, the colored people have always been recognized as the best laborers for farm work, and they have been led to believe that their services*

were appreciated, but some farmers in the State have seen fit to employ monkeys to do their work instead of colored men; therefore be it

Resolved, *That it is the sense of this meeting that all such farmers employing monkeys in lieu of colored men shall be, and are hereby, boycotted by the members of this association, and every member hereby pledges himself to stand by these resolutions.*

Resolved further, *that we call upon the colored people of every county in the State to organize, and in every association, it shall be the duty of a committee, duly appointed, to wait upon every candidate for the Legislature and ascertain his view upon this question.*

Resolved further, *that no member of the association will vote for any candidate for the Legislature who does not pledge himself to oppose the employing of monkeys instead of free colored labor.*

A Richmond paper, the *Kentucky Register*, remarked on February 25, "If the indignation against innocent Jim Parkes doesn't cease soon the Governor will have to call out 'the melish' [militia]." After weeks of not necessarily wanted worldwide notoriety, Parkes asked the *Register* to repudiate the hoax clearly. The obliging newspaper confirmed that he had no hemp field, no brother-in-law in Shelby County, no brother in Africa and "that he has no monkeys, that he never had any monkeys, and he never expects to have any monkeys." The *Louisville Times* gave the debunking revelation page-one treatment.

In time, the tale ran out of steam, but it remained in the popular consciousness for years. A reporter who interviewed Mulhattan in 1904 recounted it as one of his most memorable efforts. Like the best of Joe's hoaxes, the monkey story had the durability of cast iron and fooled people who should have known better. The noted New York evolutionary scientist Edward Payson Powell (1833–1915) read the report with great interest. According to the *Owensboro Inquirer*, Professor Powell sent J.B. Parkes photographs of various monkeys, inquiring as to which species his brother had so easily trained to do the work of humans. "Mr. Parkes turned the photographs over to Mulhattan, who replied in all earnestness." As a result, Powell's popular 1888 work on evolution, *Our Heredity from God*, repeated the ludicrous story as evidence of Darwinism's truth. The scientist opined, "I believe the cases are authentic where monkeys have been trained to field-work....I group these cases, not because they are rare exceptions, but as common illustrations of what is now being confessed by all, that animals are very human in their general intelligence." The canard remained in

Powell's book into the fifth edition, printed in 1901. The *Owensboro Inquirer* complained, "[Mulhattan] thereby has confused science and helped to ground a serious error."

Decades after Mulhattan popularized the monkey hoax via the telegraph, it occasionally reemerged, dusted off its clothes and continued its work of fooling the unwary. As late as 1934, according to Curtis MacDougall's book *Hoaxes*, "the executive editor of a publishing house wrote to the secretary of the Chamber of Commerce of Victoria [Texas] that he had been assigned to trace the origin of the story, and that the trail had led to that community. The inference of the letter was that in the interim the story had had other resurrections."

The monkey hoax provoked such a national furor that few readers noticed Mulhattan had released another creative lie from Madison County at almost the same time and even featuring the same protagonist. The *Harrodsburg Democrat* published this brief but strangely satisfying production, headlined "A Startling Phenomenon," around mid-February:

Our Madison County correspondent writes that on Sunday, about 3 p.m., a piece of ice 25 feet long by 20 feet high fell from a clear sky on the barn of Mr. James Parkes, of Madison Co., crushing the building and killing 4 head of horses. The scene of the strange incident was visited by your correspondent on Monday [yesterday] morning, and carefully examined. It is of a crystal clearness and several fish are bound in its icy embrace. One is a devil fish, an inhabitant of the deep sea; there are two sword fish, and four of a variety that your correspondent was not acquainted with. The shape of the lump is oval; the corners are supposed to have been melted in the descent. This is the hardest nut the scientists have had to crack for some time. Hundreds of people will go to see the strange visitor today before it melts away. I will send you a chunk of it by today's express. From whence came the ice?

Parkes was just lucky the free-falling iceberg didn't brain one of his monkey laborers.

CHARIVARI SHAKEDOWNS

Let's use our imaginations for a moment! Pretend you are a bride or a groom, whichever you prefer (it's none of my business), on your honeymoon. The year is around 1885 or so. This is your *first night alone* with your snugglepunkin. You just can't wait to indulge in connubial bliss—and since in 1885 moral standards were high and societal and medical penalties for engaging in premarital sex were strict, the two of you have been waiting a long time to have your love fun. Finally and at last, the moment is at hand! But suddenly you hear a voice outside: "Whooo-oop!"

Then again, closer, more voices: "Whooo-oop!"

To your dismay, people in your yard are singing with rotten voices, banging pots and pans, blowing noisemakers and making other noises limited only by their imaginations. You are experiencing an obnoxious old-timey tradition called a charivari (pronounced "shiver-ee"). The idea behind it was to disrupt a couple's honeymoon by making a distracting racket outside their house, causing maximum embarrassment and spoiling the mood as few other things can.

Writing in 1925, W.S. Kaltenbacher observed that the charivari was "an institution as old as the hills that has outlived many others." He noted that while some newlyweds in the good old days anticipated being afflicted with a charivari—some good-naturedly left treats and drinks outside for the revelers—trouble usually started when charivaris overstepped the bounds of propriety and became nuisances or even violent when the newlyweds refused to go along with the "joke" or offer treats.

Nobody is quite certain when and where the charivari originated. It was common in centuries past in Europe, especially Britain, where it was considered a means of chastising criminals, evildoers and persons not well liked by fellow citizens for whatever reason. Immigrants brought the tradition to America, but they considered it more along the lines of a practical joke than punishment. However it originated, for many decades honeymoons were wrecked by noisy jesters, not just in Kentucky but everywhere, particularly out in the country.

Looking through old papers, we find many examples from Kentucky and beyond. Consider the case of a Cherry Valley, Illinois couple who got married in November 1888. The bride, Susan McKinley, was considerably older than the groom, Charles Bowman, which drew the attention of the rabble. A reporter stated that "night has been made hideous in the vicinity of the…residence by the discordant notes of fish horns, the unearthly shrieks of the 'horse fiddle'—a diabolical contrivance composed of a dry goods box with its edges rosined and with a fence rail for a bow—and the clattering of innumerable tin pans." One alleged comedian fired a cannon in the couple's front yard, at great risk to the windows. The charivari members promised that they would go away if the groom would buy everyone liquor and let them inside to meet the bride. After four nights of ceaseless noise, the groom went to town to purchase ammunition for his duck hunting gun. He muttered something about fish horns and the coroner. There were no follow-up news stories, so let's hope the serenaders took the hint.

A charivari disturbed the honeymoon of Andrew Edwards at his Washington, Indiana home on the night of August 23, 1911, in this fashion: after he refused to buy drinks, they burst into the house and threw him downstairs. He was knocked unconscious and sustained a cut scalp, a black eye and a wounded shoulder. It was a real mood killer.

In December 1911, a crowd came to the home of newly married Frank Reynolds in Mount Eden, Spencer County, Kentucky, for the sole purpose of spoiling his honeymoon. The assembled geniuses thought that the needful thing was to "fire an anvil," a long-lost and not advisable celebratory art that involved placing gunpowder on an upside-down anvil, placing a second anvil (right side up) atop the first, and then setting off the powder to see how far into the stratosphere the top anvil would fly. In this case, a two-pound powder can ignited prematurely, and four charivarists were severely injured. The explosion probably didn't do wonders for the bride and groom either.

As late as August 1931, Mr. and Mrs. Arvo Juoni, a newlywed couple in Marengo, Wisconsin, were driven to the brink of madness by a charivari that banged pans, tooted horns and used a circular saw as a gong on their lawn nonstop for *more than two weeks*, presumably preventing the couple from scratching the cosmic itch. (Didn't any of these people have jobs?) The beleaguered honeymooners swore out warrants, but the sheriff released the partiers after he arrested them. Despite heavy rainfall, by August 6 the charivari had swollen to 150 extortionists demanding treats. The couple asked Governor La Follette for help. On August 7, 200 people were in the yard, angry because the sheriff had confiscated their tin pans, saxophones, fiddles, beer trays, washtubs, drums, iron hoops, hammers and cowbells. On this day, the weary newlyweds fed their tormentors pickled herring, coffee and cakes, and at long last they left—and good riddance. However, as they left the property, the malevolent minstrels vowed to pay a visit to another recently wed couple.

Not all victims of a charivari were good sports content to take the interruption of their marital bliss mildly, and violence erupted often enough to make one wonder why the practice continued for as long as it did. For example, we find that noisemakers interrupted a New Orleans honeymoon on April 30, 1887. The groom was a middle-aged gardener, Frederick Sallinger; the bride, Mrs. Frank, was a tasty morsel of sixty-five. Neighbors found this comical, so "a crowd assembled under the window of the bridal chamber and proceeded to salute the newly-married pair with the beating of tin pans, the tooting of horns and other accompaniments." Three serenaders broke into the house; one, Joseph Sillman, carried a club. The groom ran him through with a saber. Bystanders rushed the wounded man to a hospital, but before he passed to a better (or worse) world, he was big enough to admit that his death was his own stupid fault and asked that the law not prosecute the groom.

In another example, Levi D. Stevens, a seventy-five-year-old widower in Washington Township, near Connellsville, Pennsylvania, married his widowed sister-in-law in February 1888. A throng of highly intelligent young men showed up at Levi's house with horns, a horse fiddle, pans "and other discordant instruments." The music they made wasn't exactly symphony hall quality. After a half hour of listening to them, the elderly groom went outside and informed them, as a civilized gentleman would, that he had nothing against them personally and appreciated their attempt to entertain him—*but*, if they did not vacate the premises within ten minutes, he would settle their hash. They gave him a rousing sarcastic cheer and kept playing. At the ten-minute deadline, the groom came out the door, jerked the tin horn out of the leader's hand and struck him between the eyes with it. The "musician" crumpled unconscious to the ground. Then Levi took the battered horn and used it to beat two others into submission. He picked up a horse fiddle player, who had a reputation as a bully, and threw him at another youth who had been using a stick and a tin can as instruments. One of this pair had his wind knocked out; when he recovered his breath, he shouted, "Murder! Murder!" At this point, the wiseguys scattered, but the groom seized the collar of one who wasn't quite fast enough and hurled him over a fence. We learn all this from a charivari member who had the good sense to scale the fence and observe the proceedings from a safe distance.

Newlywed Martin Phillips took his bride home to Lopez Island, Washington, in December 1889, and before you could say "delayed consummation" the house was surrounded by a crowd of off-key crooners. Martin aimed a double-barreled shotgun loaded with slugs at them and fired, after which two members met His Bony Highness. That ended the festivities, and Martin spent his honeymoon not canoodling with his new wife, as he desired, but in jail protesting that he had warned the charivari repeatedly that he would shoot if they didn't leave.

A farmer named William Ingraham got married at Evergreen, Alabama, on March 22, 1894. He and his bride found their romantic evening disturbed by humorists with cowbells, tin pans "and similar doleful and noisy instruments." The farmer registered his displeasure by tossing an axe into the crowd. It severed the spinal cord of a lad named Jimmy Dickson. Dickson's soul flew to its native home like a gentle dove, and the farmer went straight to jail.

"Half-witted" Richard Webster of Wellington, Kansas, found his wedding night of November 20, 1894, ruined by a boisterous charivari. He fired a revolver, killing two men.

Sometimes members of a charivari committed violence against each other. George Dunowirth got married in Pendleton County, Kentucky, on August 19, 1897, and the usual mob of idiots—uh, people with a sparkling sense of humor—went to his house to do their stuff. Not content with making a cacophony with musical instruments, they also brought guns. Orville Courtney accidentally shot Marsh Elrod in the back. Next morning, the remorseful slayer shot himself. Similarly, "a crowd of young people were creating pandemonium by every imaginable means" on the night of June 9, 1913, outside the home of newlywed James Goode near Caledonia, Trigg County, Kentucky. Several fired pistols, greatly to the detriment of Terry McGee, one of their party.

In February 1915, a group of young women went to visit a newly married couple at Cow Creek in Lee County, Kentucky. They were bringing the bride a present, but a relative mistook them for a charivari and opened fire. Ten women were injured, none seriously, but the story well illustrates the hatred charivaris incurred.

Posey Beckham married his wife for the second time on June 29, 1915. One might think a re-marriage would be of little interest to a charivari, but troublesome troubadours surrounded Beckham's Howell, Indiana home ere nightfall. They demanded a treat. He told them to go to an undesirable location well known for its balmy climate. They tossed rocks through his windows. Posey retaliated with a rifle shot, fatally injuring an eight-year-old boy.

Trave Robards of Sebree, Webster County, Kentucky, had better things in mind than spending his wedding night, December 6, 1915, listening to young boys yowling in his yard. He fired a shot in the air and then lowered the gun. It went off a second time and hit William Deering in the legs. Trave swore that the second time was just an accident.

You didn't even have to be recently married to be targeted by a charivari; sometimes they just thought it was amusing to deprive people of sleep. Reuben Parrish, a "hard-working colored man" who lived at Floyd and Pearl Streets in Louisville, was annoyed on the morning of February 9, 1898, by a crowd that got its jollies by singing "Sweet Rosie O'Grady" at him. Reuben asked them to shut up and go away. They responded by belting out a popular song from 1897 titled "I Guess that Will Hold You for a While." Reuben fired point blank at the group while remarking with lacerating wit, "I guess that will hold you *all* for a while." No one was injured, but police arrested Reuben, much to his indignation. The *Courier-Journal* hinted in a roundabout fashion that it was on Reuben's side, remarking editorially, "A man who had a chance to shoot at such a party and missed the whole layout ought to be arrested."

Those are just a few examples of the violence caused by past ruffians in desperate need of entertainment. If I may speculate, perhaps charivaris inspired the tradition of honeymoon vacations. At one time, most newlyweds honeymooned at home, as clearly shown in these stories, but the farther away a couple traveled, the less likely they would face wedding night persecution.

Gradually the practice died out—who knows when or how? The charivari is no more and is so extinct that readers finding references to them in old books and newspapers have to look up the definition and are surprised to discover that their ancestors were so annoying. Readers also naturally wonder whether mobs so targeted their own great-grandparents.

There are many old-time customs it would be nice to revive, but let's hope this one stays dead.

PROFESSOR TOBIN BAFFLES LOUISVILLE, THEN THE WORLD

Professor Thomas William Tobin is an unjustly neglected figure from Louisville history. Born in London, England, in January 1844, he became a noted chemist, architect, inventor, scientist and lecturer at London's Polytechnic Institute. If Tobin is remembered at all, it is among professional magicians for developing several stage illusions that are still used. For his achievements in magic, an association of magicians placed a monument on Tobin's unmarked grave in Cave Hill Cemetery on March 22, 2018. Louisville native and magician Lance Burton was instrumental in getting Tobin this recognition and led the Broken Wand Ceremony, a ritual performed at the graves of conjurers by fellow performers.

Tobin's gravestone lists his four most noted illusions. One was the Cabinet of Proteus (1864), described on the Magicpedia website: "People appear and disappear from a large cabinet that has folding doors in front and an upright pillar that extends from top to bottom inside. At the top of the pillar is usually a lamp which illuminates the inside." In Palingenesia (1872), the performer seems to cut an assistant into pieces and then reassemble him; Houdini incorporated it into a Broadway show in 1925. The Oracle of Delphi (1865) is described by Magicpedia as being a "sort of cross between Tobin's other successful illusions, The Sphinx and Pepper's Ghost." (Tobin and his friend Professor John Henry Pepper developed Pepper's Ghost. It involved making a ghost seem to appear onstage by using cleverly placed mirrors.) His most celebrated trick was the Sphinx Illusion (1865), in which a seemingly disembodied head roosts in a cabinet

on a tabletop and converses with spectators. Your local community spook house employs the illusion every Halloween.

In 1872, Pepper and Tobin took their illusions on tour in America. The professors did not meet with the financial success they expected and broke up the act when they reached Louisville. Pepper sold his magic apparatus to Colonel Bennett H. Young for $700 and returned to England. Tobin, however, chose to remain. He made many prominent friends quickly, including Colonel Young, who found Tobin a job around 1874 as chair of the Chemistry Department at a brand-new institution of higher learning in Richmond called Central University (now Eastern Kentucky University). Tobin's experiments there made him well known throughout the state. In 1880, he moved back to Louisville and became a nationally renowned scientist at the city's Polytechnic Society on Fourth Street. Among many other accomplishments, he was one of the first persons in America to cook with electricity.

However, in Louisville the creator of magic tricks became notorious for a different sort of trick. On May 25, 1882, the professor entered the dining room of the Fifth Avenue Hotel and announced to acquaintances that he had created a puzzle. He drew a curious figure on the back of a menu:

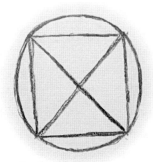

"Now," said Tobin, "The object is to trace this figure of the circumscribed square without removing the pencil from the paper or retracing any of the lines." He said he would give $50 to the first person who could do it. The equivalent in modern currency is more than $1,000, so the prize wasn't chump change.

It looked simple enough, so of course everyone present thought it would be a snap. A *Courier-Journal* reporter who was present described the result when they tried:

> [All] *were hard at the puzzle. The success was about uniform; each man found himself one line short. Again and again the same thing was accomplished, but no one was successful....The seeds of pernicious curiosity had been sown and soon bore fruit....Every now and then some fellow would pull out his pencil and try for a second or two to follow the problem, meanwhile casting furtive glances at the instigator of the mischief who sat explaining the mathematical principles of the thing to his neighbor.*

No one could solve it. Within a few days, the hotel reverberated with the gentle swears of hooked, hollow-eyed beings who took the challenge and failed repeatedly. Some tried working the puzzle during meals, leaving their sustenance neglected. Hotel residents would beam with joy, thinking they were successful, only to sink in despair upon finding they still had one line undrawn. A reporter said every scrap of paper in the building bore the figure, drawn by discouraged would-be puzzle solvers, whom the writer depicted as "wretched victims of [the] baleful diagram" soon to be housed at the lunatic asylum. "It's enough to drive a wooden Indian mad," remarked a disconsolate desk clerk.

The reporter, after noting that papers bearing the puzzle covered the hotel's floors, asked one of the "used-up" men, Rowan Buchanan, how long he intended to work at it. "Until the year 1990 if necessary," he retorted. "If we die in the attempt, you will find memoranda for our obituaries on the mantel." (Another baffled hotel resident was the ironically nicknamed State Treasurer "Honest Dick" Tate, who in a few years would pull off his own magical disappearing act by absconding to parts unknown with a significant chunk of Kentucky's money.)

On the plus side, Professor Tobin promised the sufferers he would soon reveal the answer and put them out of their misery. On May 30, the *Courier-Journal* ran a picture of Tobin's puzzle, figuring that other people would like to join the fun. The net effect was that the frustration over solving it was no longer confined to a single building but loosed on the entire city. The next day, the paper ran one of those delightful multi-part headlines common in the era:

> *In Hoc Signo Vinces* [In this sign you will conquer]. *The Tobinsicosis Epidemic Still Continues Unabated and the Fever Is at Its Height. Strong Men Weep and Tear Their Hair over the Bisected Circumscribed Square. A Thousand Melancholy People Call on the Instigator of the Baleful Business. A Number of Ingenious Solutions, None of Which Entitle the Authors to the Prize. Fitting for the Lunatic Asylum.*

The writer included anecdotes demonstrating how Professor Tobin's puzzle was the city's obsession: "Interest in the Tobin puzzle has extended to the utmost parts of the city, and there is scarcely a man, woman, or child to be found who has not devoted all leisure time, since the appearance of the *Courier-Journal* yesterday morning, to a solution of the problem that proved so absorbing." Children chalked the figure on the city's walls and pavements—even, fittingly, on the *Courier-Journal* building. The newspaper received alleged solutions by mail—by June 3, they numbered five hundred.

One person offered a solution based on nautical reasoning. A woman demurely suggested that she deserved forty-five dollars of the fifty-dollar prize since she *almost* figured it out. All of these ingenious persons were ingeniously wrong.

"Up and down Main Street clerks tore their hair and proprietors swore," said a reporter. Many smug citizens claimed to have solved the problem but were unable to duplicate their success before witnesses. Observers saw Judge Dupuy drawing the sign in the margin of the daily court docket. Another dignified man from legal circles, Judge Kincaid, drew the figure in the air with his cane as he strolled down a city street. On the other end of the social spectrum, a drunkard chalked the puzzle on the back of a fellow tippler. Just as modern bosses complain about lack of productivity caused by workers fiddling with cellphones or the internet rather than doing the work for which they are paid, Louisville's bosses of 1882 claimed that employees were too obsessed with Tobin's puzzle to earn their wages.

Many telephoned the professor at the Polytechnic demanding a solution. Others were not content merely to phone and went in person. They came by the dozens on May 30. The assistant librarian decided to keep count late in the afternoon and said that between 3:00 p.m. and 5:30 p.m., 211 distraught persons came seeking relief. The librarian estimated that, in all, about 1,000 people came that day in search of Tobin, who hid behind the double-bolted doors of the Polytechnic's laboratory. A *Courier-Journal* reporter found the professor and beseeched him for the answer. Tobin gave the journalist a reply in learned-sounding algebraical gibberish.

Then the advertiser for H.A. Witherspoon's clothing store, knowing a good publicity gimmick when he saw one, got in on the act. Witherspoon's re-created the by-now-notorious image on page one of the June 1 *Courier-Journal* with the caption "Prize Puzzle! We Can't Solve It but Offer a $15 Suit of Clothes for First Solution." Professor Tobin was to decide the best solution. Witherspoon's cagily added that *another* puzzle was how they managed to sell high-quality clothing at such low prices: "There is a prize in each purchase."

Out-of-state newspapers duplicated the drawing, and the puzzle became a national fad. Then, on June 4, came the solution—or, to be more precise, the non-solution. After keeping Louisvillians and other Americans in a froth of misery for days, the *Courier-Journal* confessed that Tobin's puzzle was a hoax—"The best hoax of the season." The solution was that there *was* no solution!

Solving the problem under the conditions set by the professor required one to draw a square and cross combination without retracing a line or lifting the pencil off the paper—an utter impossibility, as a few attempts will demonstrate. It was as hopeless, said the *Courier-Journal*, as trying to take hold of your bootstraps and lift yourself off the floor. Tobin was sublimely confident offering a fifty-dollar prize because he knew no one could win. (Note to any reader who has solved it while reading this book: *you are a genius!*)

Were a newspaper to pull off a similar stunt today—publicizing a hefty prize for a brainteaser with no answer—various soreheads who really wanted that prize would probably slap it with nuisance lawsuits. It appears, however, that the folks of 1882 enjoyed the trick and didn't mind being "sold"—at least, there is no record of anyone complaining to the *Courier-Journal*.

The aftermath of the revelation tells something of the human condition—and it isn't very flattering to us. Even after the *Courier-Journal* made it clear that Professor Tobin's puzzle was unsolvable, some people refused to believe it and continued straining for a solution. The *Washington Critic* and the *Philadelphia Times* both reprinted the puzzle and said that citizens of their respective cities were going nuts. The *Courier-Journal* reported on June 11, long after it let the cat out of the bag, that mail from people still trying to solve the puzzle inundated its office and Professor Tobin. The paper observed on July 2, before reprinting a postcard from Natchez, Mississippi, begging for the solution:

> *Even after all the assurances that the problem was unsolvable, many people are hard at work upon it, and not a day passes that does not bring with it half a dozen inquiries [as] to supposed solutions. New York went wild over it, and the aesthetic Boston followed. Buxom Baltimore girls pouted their pretty lips over it, and underpaid government clerks fretted in Washington and drew it upon Uncle Sam's vouchers. Wicked Chicago cursed it, and lazy New Orleans discussed it over cigarettes and café noir. It smelled the pine odors of the Maine forests and inhaled the pure, free air of the Sierras, but still nobody was able to do it.... [The puzzle is] gradually fastening its clutches on hamlets, remote country villages, obscure crossroads, and Cincinnati. Dr. Tobin is of the opinion that the Zulus will trace it in the burning sands of South Africa before it is finally consigned to oblivion.*

Depending on your point of view, these readers' efforts to solve an enigma they were informed was an unsolvable hoax were a tribute to either human indomitability or impregnable human stupidity.

Little more than a year after perpetrating his practical joke, Professor Tobin died at St. Joseph's Infirmary in Louisville on August 4, 1883, accompanied by two friends: Dr. Thomas Royall, a lifelong acquaintance from England, and Noah Saunders, a black man who was Tobin's lab assistant. The professor had wasted away from tuberculosis, the same disease that took his mother and all of his brothers and sisters. In his last moments, his thoughts were on his beloved Polytechnic Society. His body lay in state there next day. The board of trustees at Cave Hill Cemetery deemed it a great honor to bury him there, although why his grave was unmarked for so long is a mystery.

Tobin's obituary said many nice things about him and his accomplishments. However, no doubt many remembered him primarily as the man who afflicted first Louisville and then the world at large with an unsolvable conundrum. Perhaps the associated magicians of America should engrave the puzzle on the back of his tombstone, so that future generations may weep with exasperation over it.

THE SECOND
BEETHOVEN'S FIRST

Sometimes musicologists state that the first American performance of
a Beethoven work took place in Lexington, Kentucky. Close but no
cheroot: according to music historian Michael Broyles, the American debut
of Beethoven's music was in South Carolina in 1805. However, the *third*
Beethoven performance in the United States did occur in Lexington! Third
counts for something, right?

Jacob Eckhard conducted the South Carolina performance in Charleston
on April 10, 1805. No one knows which Beethoven work he performed, but
Broyles suggests that it "was probably the first movement of a symphony"—
if so, then it almost certainly was the Symphony No. 1, as it was the most
accessible and least complex of the three Beethoven had composed by 1805.
It must have gone over well, since in 1806 the conductor opened and closed
an Easter celebration concert with more Beethoven.

Lexington, then, can claim being the location of the third performance
of a Beethoven work in America. If Eckhard did conduct the Symphony
No. 1 back in 1805, then Lexington witnessed the second American
performance of the symphony. The event took place on November
12, 1817, and the conductor was Austrian immigrant Anthony Philip
Heinrich. A local paper, the *Kentucky Gazette*, ran an advertisement in the
November 8 issue:

> GRAND CONCERT. *A.P. Henreich* [sic], *by request of his Musical friends and
> others, respectfully acquaints the Ladies and Gentlemen of Lexington that*

on Wednesday Evening next, 12ᵗʰ inst., at Keene and Lanphear's Assembly Room, he will give a PUBLIC CONCERT assisted by the Professionals and Amateurs of this place.

It will be noted that the ad misspelled the conductor's name and didn't mention that he intended to perform Beethoven. Fortunately, another Lexington paper, the *Kentucky Reporter*, ran a more detailed notice confirming it; in fact, it was the first piece listed. We also learn from the ad that admission was one dollar per head, quite pricey at the time.

Forget any visions you might have of the mighty strains of the Symphony No. 1 echoing through a fine early Kentucky concert hall; the performance took place at Postlethwaite's Tavern at Main and Limestone, current location of the Lexington Public Library.

Heinrich must have been an above-average musician, as he later helped found the New York Philharmonic Society. However, disappointingly for posterity, while the *Gazette* and the *Reporter* ran ads for the concert, they did not print reviews, leaving us to wonder what Lexingtonians of 1817 thought of Beethoven. It is a question that will blight our lives forever. According to legend, Beethoven shook his fist at a thunderstorm when on his deathbed, but maybe he was really shaking his fist in memory of those Kentuckians who didn't review his symphony.

CHARLES MANSON SURPRISES AN IDIOT

When the news got out that Charles Manson had died in prison on November 19, 2017, a wave of nostalgia hit me. You might call it nostalgia. Thirty-two years before, I had written Manson a letter, more or less as a joke, and he actually replied.

Back in the late summer of 1985, I was a teenage bonehead just starting my freshman year at Berea College in Berea, Kentucky. Recently, I had read in a newspaper that Charles Manson, leader of the infamous California cult of late 1960s murderous hippies, whiled away his spare time in prison by making humanoid dolls out of yarn from unraveled socks. One evening, after telling everyone at the cafeteria dinner table about Manson's folksy pastime, I chortled, "Wouldn't it be great if I asked him for one and he actually gave it to me?"

Everyone hooted and jeered, "Yeah, sure! Right!" I took this as a challenge. Next day, I went to the library and found the address of the prison where I had read Manson was imprisoned (it turned out to be outdated information). Then I wrote him an *exceedingly* polite letter, being careful not to mention the Beatles, telling him I had read about his interesting sock dolls in the paper and asking if I might buy one. I included a self-addressed stamped envelope, because that's the polite thing to do, and mailed the letter. I did not really expect a reply. Surely, Charles Manson had better, or worse, things to do than write to a college kid?

A few weeks passed. Other things occupied my mind, such as trying to pass a remedial math class, longing to impress a certain brunette, wondering

where my childhood went, foolishly—although temporarily—turning my back on essential truths and being sublimely confident that R.E.M. would never, *ever* make a bad album.

One fine day in September, I went to my CPO (college post office) box and pulled out a yellow envelope postmarked September 16, 1985. On second glance, I noticed it had one of those pre-addressed adhesive labels in the upper-left corner—and the sender's name was Charles M. Manson. On the label, he handwrote his prison number and his new prison address in Tamal, California. I almost swallowed my tongue. I remember thinking, *This is the coolest, but dumbest, thing I've ever done!* When I opened the envelope with shaking hands, I found a handwritten letter from Manson, who claimed to have sent one of his homemade sock dolls, although the doll was not in the envelope. It read exactly as follows, with my explanatory comments in brackets:

> *KMC—Here is a Mansonite.* [Smiley face, because even mass-murdering cult leaders think smileys are cute.] *I call them that*

because people say VODO [voodoo] + *they are NOT VODO or JUJU or nothing like that—There are just a Hobby—I don't charge for them because Im not in traid—They take a lot of time to make but how much can a sox be worth—Once in a while Ill just send one here + ther Ive got them all over the world they git on tryps by them selves—if you want to send some $ a good friend of mine is in prison Broke + you can send him what you think its worth* [prisoner's first name redacted] *Wilson.* [Address ditto] *it combs out + you can set it to hang or stand—His name is Sandie my little Mansonites call him Big Sandie because my Grandad was the condutur on the C + O on the Big Sandy Run on the C + O + This in KY he will be in—Ride Easy Charles Manson*

Manson told me the autobiographical business about his grandfather's having been a conductor on the C&O at Big Sandy at a time when the fact was not generally known. According to James M. Gifford, who has done research into the famous criminal's ancestry, Manson's grandfather Charles Milles Maddox held that job until his death in 1931.

Manson spent considerable time writing to people while in prison, but he was very choosy about his correspondents. In one case, a man had to write Manson fifty letters before he answered. Why did he decide to write to me? I never figured that one out and was too nervous to ask, but perhaps it was the Kentucky connection. I found the whole thing pretty scary, especially since he signed his name by drawing a swastika over the *s* in Manson. I was sufficiently foolhardy and curious to send another polite letter stating that the doll wasn't in the envelope and asking if perhaps somebody stole it. I also truthfully told Manson that I sent a small sum of money to this Wilson fellow but that the letter had come back marked "Return to sender." Manson sent another letter, postmarked September 26. This rambling epistle was longer and scarier and covered two sides of a page. I couldn't help noticing that the letter rhymed in places (Manson was a frustrated songwriter and Beatle wannabe):

Mc Q., It takes any where from 30 to 50 hours + some times longer to make this type of doll—That's not the hard part, the hard part is that in the hole the type of nylon used to touch the effect that makes the doll unique is not permitted—Gitting to doll to the place I send it is another hill all together as the crooks that lie about almost everything are not the least bit honest with them selves so as the world turns the out law becomes the law + the law does become the out law—a guy sold a doll *once for $395.00 (That's a strange price) but you can see when I don't sell them they are priceless HA HA—I don't think the name being on the envelope ment anything—it* [the doll] *didn't git out of the prison—I don't have another one to send right now + Im not in a place where I can do much of anything—WHEN was then as its always been, but when as then or once again—if—I remember + git the chance to git one through the confusion they play prison + justice with I will send to you—also the name is rulled by CDC* [California Department of Corrections] *to be put on the letter with number + place so Im held to obay the laws but I don't think there is anyone to hold the law to obay ther own laws—so that cuts down chances of gitting the big sandy running true—Everything I do, or say, wright or yell is riped off for T.V.'s in other names, for other games as first came the law's + there were no laws to be out from. So as it turns around again + you can see the doll was honest = it didn't git to you SO as the real story's of real deals on real wheels for AIR, WATER TREES, + wild life, is covered for money + the elusion of power tryps—Im not much of a paper word wrighter so I don't want to git in to a letter wrighting tryp—If you want to know anything wright the Butcher Man of Willsons blade + for a few bucks he will wright letters all day—See how nice I seem + I smile now for the crash—DON'T wright me no more, Im not a pen pal—This boy been out of them hills a long time + Im still there but NOT in no school Im with the earth + things of the Earth—Easy Charles Manson*

I never found out who the "Butcher Man of Willson's Blade" was, and I certainly didn't ask. But perhaps Manson felt remorse about ending his letter so bluntly because right out of the blue he sent a third, unasked-for letter postmarked October 10. It contained three Polaroid pictures (how did he get access to a Polaroid?) showing some of his "Mansonite" dolls hanging on a line. What colorful, jolly little buggers they were! One picture showed what appeared to be a blue prison uniform hanging next to the sock dolls. A letter was enclosed that read simply, "Some Side ways pictures—Ill git you one of this dolls when I can."

By now, I was jumpy about the whole Charles Manson business and didn't care if I never got one of his sock dolls. Then, in December, a large manila envelope arrived from a West Coast man claiming to be Manson's friend and legal representative. Now here was something I had not considered when planning my lame-brained stunt: of course Manson couldn't get to me because he was safely in prison, but he had friends—even followers!—

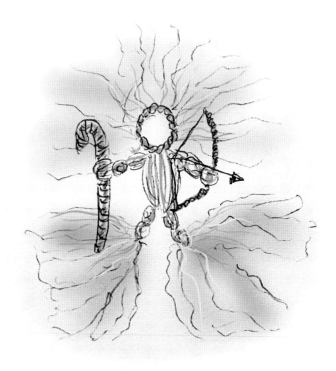

on the outside. The envelope contained one of the "Mansonites" depicted in the Polaroids. It wasn't "Big Sandy." Rather, the sender told me the doll's name was "Little Coup," as in *coup d'état*. If seen from an objective point of view, it was quite a work of art. It was a humanlike figure made of blended green, white, orange and red nylon and it was holding a coup stick and a bow and arrow.

The West Coast man's stationery featured what I took to be a Satanic symbol and ended with the words: "Charlie evidently thinks very highly of you, or he wouldn't have asked me to send you this doll...and I would like to know more about you myself." The bottom of his letter featured an indecipherable handwritten two-word phrase, one word of which looked to my panicky eyes very much like "devil."

This was followed soon by a letter from the man's wife (more Satanic-looking symbols at the top of the page—it's a real attention-getter, let me tell you!). Her letter was very pleasant and chatty, but it ended with a distressing reference to Manson's imprisoned disciple Squeaky Fromme. Not long afterward, Manson sent a final letter reading, "Mc, Did you git the Mansonite [Smiley face] you got to comb it + set it—Easy Manson."

By this point, I had learned a valuable lesson about how a little dare can get out of hand. I sent a very, very, *very* nice letter to the West Coast couple explaining that I wasn't really sure why Charlie had taken such a shine to me unless it was because I happened to be from Kentucky, and all I had really wanted was one of the dolls for its value as a curiosity. I never heard again from them or Manson, but for years afterward, the very sight of a hippie would make me blanch from fear that one of "the Family" had come to get me. In 1987, Squeaky Fromme temporarily broke out of her West Virginia prison cell, and I was a very nervous lad for a few days. I thought I might find her in the dorm lobby one morning, wearing that silly elf hat of hers and muttering, "Charlie says you're cool, man." Take my advice: next time you see an article in the papers about a mass murderer's handcrafts, turn to "Jumble, That Scrambled Word Game" on the funny pages instead.

For a few years, I wondered if I had been the victim of an elaborate hoax. However, in June 1987, the *Lexington Herald-Leader* ran a few stories about a theater group in Owensboro that had written to a number of celebrities asking for personal items it could auction off. One of these celebrities was Manson. He sent them some dolls and a letter or two. A controversy immediately arose because some people felt it would be in bad taste to auction the memorabilia. The paper reprinted a few of the letters, and the spelling, syntax and philosophy were identical to the letters I had received.

Today, my four handwritten letters from Manson, his Polaroid photos and Little Coup the sock doll are stored in a bank safety deposit box, which I hope has a lining thick enough to contain their emanations.

BIBLIOGRAPHY

LITTLE-KNOWN LINCOLN STORIES

Chrisman, Francis Leon. "Lincoln's Famous Hat." *Louisville Courier-Journal*, February 9, 1896, III, 2.

Cigrand, Prof. Bernard J. "The True and Authentic Story of Lincoln's Substitute." *Louisville Courier-Journal*, February 12, 1911, IV, 2.

Haskin, Frederic J. "Stories of Abraham Lincoln." *Louisville Courier-Journal*, February 12, 1907, 4.

Johnston, J. Stoddard. "Abraham Lincoln's Duel...." *Louisville Courier-Journal*, January 29, 1899, III, 3.

Louisville Courier-Journal. "Abraham Lincoln's Ax." May 29, 1903, 4.

————. "An Abraham Lincoln Story." November 10, 1912, II, 13.

————. "At a Sale of Autographs in Boston...." November 29, 1879, 2.

————. "Boyhood of Lincoln Spent in Southern Indiana." October 19, 1902, II, 10.

————. "Cabinet Made by Lincoln Saved from Burning." December 16, 1907, 3.

————. "Lincoln Appreciated Good Socks." April 9, 1902, 3.

————. "Lincoln Car Sold." August 5, 1903, 2.

————. "Lincoln Died on Booth's Bed." November 12, 1895, 2.

————. "Lincoln Made Him a Cane." August 17, 1907, 6.

————. "Lincoln's Autograph More Valued than Washington's." November 11, 1905, 7.

————. "Lincoln's Car Rotting in the Union Pacific Yard...." February 6, 1897, 10.

————. "Lincoln's Dictionary Given to Society." October 8, 1912, 2.

————. "Odds and Ends." August 12, 1906, III, 3.

————. "On Dit." September 26, 1903, 6.

————. "Overcoat Worn by Lincoln Is Missing." November 8, 1904, 3.

———. "Propose Monument to Lincoln's Substitute." February 4, 1910, 8.

———. "Shields and Lincoln." May 12, 1878, 1.

———. "Thomas Lincoln and Nancy Hanks Plighted Faith…." January 16, 1901, 2.

———. "An 'Unofficial' Bride of the White House." February 18, 1906, I, 4.

———. "Veteran Poses." August 28, 1911, 3.

———. "Wilkes Booth's Clothes." March 29, 1896, II, 5.

Patroni. "Speaking Of." *Louisville Courier-Journal*, December 7, 1897, 4.

Riverside (CA) Daily Press. "White House Bride Whom Lincoln Gave Away…." February 12, 1929, 11.

Wood, Henry Cleveland. "The Man Who United the Parents of Lincoln." *Louisville Courier-Journal*, April 11, 1897, 7.

KENTUCKY GHOST TOWNS

Granard

Louisville Courier-Journal. "In Name Only." August 22, 1897, IV, 4.

———. "Saloons and Groceries." March 9, 1914, 5.

Martinsville

Louisville Courier-Journal. "A Lost Village." November 2, 1902, II, 3.

Rennick, Robert M. *Kentucky Place Names*. Lexington: University Press of Kentucky, 1984.

Florence Station

Louisville Courier-Journal. "Village Soon to Be Off the Map." July 17, 1905, 4.

Lystra

Giovannoli, H. "Lost City of Lystra." *Louisville Courier-Journal*, September 12, 1897, IV, 1.

Louisville Courier-Journal. "Lost Cities." February 17, 1902, 6.

McGill, Anna Blanche. "Lystra—Kentucky's Dream City." *Louisville Courier-Journal*, October 19, 1919, magazine section, 11.

Beallsborough

Louisville Courier-Journal. "Lost Cities." February 17, 1902, 6.

Mortonsville

Louisville Courier-Journal. "Kentucky Ghost Town Has 104th Birthday." March 1, 1939, II, 1.

Rennick, Robert M. *Kentucky Place Names.* Lexington: University Press of Kentucky, 1984.

Milford

Clay, Green. "A Bitten Ear Helped Make a Ghost Town." *Louisville Courier-Journal,* December 10, 1939, magazine section.

Airdrie

Kaltenbacher, Will. "Huge Meteorite in Kentucky Soil." *Louisville Courier-Journal,* September 28, 1930, VII, 8.

Louisville Courier-Journal. "Kentucky's Famous Old Deserted City." February 5, 1911, IV, 1.

Rennick, Robert M. *Kentucky Place Names.* Lexington: University Press of Kentucky, 1984.

Mortalles

Louisville Courier-Journal. "End of 'Mysterious City.'" February 3, 1914, 2.

———. "Kentucky Marsh Staked for New Utopia." April 23, 1911, IV, 1.

———. "Magic City Under Hammer." February 13, 1914, 3.

———. "Mysterious City May Quench Hoosiers' Thirst." July 1, 1918, 1.

———. "Opening of Dream City Saloon Will Be Fought." July 16, 1918, 3.

TWO MISSING PERSONS

Willis E. Smith

Louisville Courier-Journal. "All Lexington Dazed by Story." October 2, 1908, 1.

———. "Attempt to Unravel the Smith Mystery." December 28, 1908, 1.

———. "Believes Brother Was Murdered." October 5, 1908, 1.

———. "Boxcar Theory Will Not Down." October 3, 1908, 1.

———. "Brother of Missing Student Makes Pathetic Appeal." October 11, 1908, IV, 1.

———. "College Student on Missing List." September 28, 1908, 3.

———. "End of a Mystery." Editorial, January 1, 1909, 4.

———. "Grand Jury Making Close Investigation…." October 19, 1908, 3.

———. "Grand Jury on the Smith Disappearance." October 14, 1908, 9.

———. "Investigation Brings No Information...." October 10, 1908, 4.

———. "Lack of Discipline at State University." October 30, 1908, 1.

———. "Leaves Work of Clearing Up Smith Mystery Unfinished." October 25, 1908, I, 5.

———. "Lexington Rumors." Editorial, October 7, 1908, 6.

———. "Man Found in a Freight Car." October 6, 1908, 2.

———. "Missing College Student Turns Up at Owensboro." December 31, 1908, 1+.

———. "Missing Smith: Decatur, Ill....." October 10, 1908, 3.

———. "The Missing Student." September 23, 1909, 8.

———. "Mock Funeral for the 'Missing Student.'" September 23, 1911, 3.

———. "Mountain Boy Who Came to College at Lexington Missing." September 26, 1908, 3.

———. "Movement Started by Students to Dig...." December 30, 1908, 7.

———. "Murder Theory." September 29, 1908, 7.

———. "Mystery Grows Regarding Disappearance of Smith...." November 5, 1908, 7.

———. "New Life Put into Search...." October 27, 1908, 7.

———. "No Romance in Willis Smith's Running Away...." January 1, 1909, 6.

———. "Not Missing Student." November 6, 1908, 4.

———. "Possible Clew [sic], Smith Mystery." October 8, 1908, 8.

———. "A Professor's Publicity." Editorial, December 30, 1908, 4.

———. "Resents Interest in Missing Student's Case." December 29, 1908, 2.

———. "Smith Family Give Up Hope." October 5, 1908, 1+.

———. "Smith Mystery." October 17, 1908, 4.

———. "Smith Mystery Bring Many Amateur Detectives...." October 24, 1908, 9.

———. "Smith's Body Lies in Sewer." December 27, 1908, IV, 1.

———. "Stories of the Town." October 30, 1908, 4.

———. "Student Smith Still Missing." October 7, 1908, 4.

———. "Student Still Missing." September 30, 1908, 4.

———. "Twelfth Night; Still Missing." October 4, 1908, I, 1.

———. "Two Smiths at Same Time." October 9, 1908, 5.

———. "University Faculty Glad Smith Turned Up." December 31, 1908, 1.

———. "Wandered Off." December 30, 1908, 5.

Ella Rogers

Briney, John. "When the Lights Went Out." *Louisville Courier-Journal*, September 15, 1957, magazine section, 7+.

Coady, Jean Haverton. "What Ever Happened to Ella McDowell Rogers?" *Louisville Courier-Journal*, September 11, 1978, C-1.

Louisville Courier-Journal. "Ashes Guarded in Rogers Mystery." November 27, 1928, 1+.

———. "Blood Stains Found in Rogers Case." January 5, 1929, 1+.

———. "Body Found in Park Here Is Identified." February 17, 1929, I, 1.

————. "Death Declaration in Rogers Case Is Aim." October 10, 1935, 15.

————. "Harned Denies Break with Widow." November 28, 1928, 1+.

————. "Haynes Admits Serving Term." December 28, 1928, 1+.

————. "Haynes Case Passed Again." February 2, 1929, 5.

————. "Haynes Goes Back to Prison Friday." May 3, 1929, 5.

————. "Haynes Is Grilled by Otte, Cops." February 24, 1929, I, 1.

————. "Haynes Is Sure of Prison Term." December 29, 1928, 1.

————. "Haynes Trial Is Continued Again." February 28, 1929, 17.

————. "Housewife Tells of Sending Copy of Will...." January 31, 1947, 15.

————. "Human Bones Found Here in New Grave." December 4, 1928, 1.

————. "Information Asked About Rogers Will." February 1, 1929, 10.

————. "Judgment Awarded Against Mrs. Rogers." March 9, 1930, I, 1.

————. "Kin, Friend Differ on Rogers Clew [sic]." November 25, 1928, I, 1+.

————. "Kin Named Executor of Rogers Estate." October 16, 1935, 5.

————. "Little Is Found by Rogers Test." December 2, 1928, I, 1+.

————. "Mrs. Ella Rogers Is Held Legally Dead." October 12, 1935, 1+.

————. "Mrs. Rogers' Diamond Ring Hunted Here." January 6, 1929, I. 1.

————. "Mystery Case Clew [sic] Is False." November 19, 1928, 1.

————. "Negro in Rogers Case Paroled." August 17, 1929, 1.

————. "Not Mrs. Rogers Either." February 19, 1929, 28.

————. "Officers Drop Mystery Case." December 5, 1928, 3.

————. "One Phase of the Parole Law...." Editorial, December 31, 1928, 4.

————. "$1000 Reward Out in Rogers Case." November 24, 1928, 1+.

————. "Prosecutor Probes Rogers Case...." November 21, 1928, 1+.

————. "Radio Hunt for Widow Starts." November 26, 1928, 1+.

————. "Rogers Case Again Revived." February 6, 1929, 4.

————. "Rogers Case Revived Here." December 27, 1928, 1.

————. "Rogers Case Test Begun by Chemist." December 1, 1928, 1+.

————. "Rogers Estate Curator Named." July 22, 1932, 5.

————. "Rogers Estate Curator Replaced." July 29, 1932, 26.

————. "Rogers Estate Windup Sought." October 11, 1935, I, 5.

————. "Rogers Former Janitor Arrested." November 23, 1928, 1+.

————. "Rogers Mystery Probe Is Pushed." November 29, 1928, 1+.

————. "Rogers Probe Resumed Here." December 23, 1928, I, 1+.

————. "Rogers Puzzle Still Unsolved." December 3, 1928, 1.

————. "Rogers Rumor Is Called 'Wild.'" March 10, 1931, 18.

————. "Search for Mrs. Rogers Is Unavailing." November 18, 1928, I, 1.

————. "Skeleton of Woman Found Near Tracks." August 24, 1937, I, 5.

————. "Vanished." Editorial, November 25, 1928, V, 4.

————. "Widow Here Vanishes; Fear Felt." November 17, 1928, 1+.

————. "Yarberry Finds Clew [sic]...." November 30, 1928, 1+.

BIBLIOGRAPHY

DON'T GIVE UP THE DAY JOB

Hearn, Daniel Allen. *Legal Executions in Illinois, Indiana, Iowa, Kentucky, and Missouri: A Comprehensive Registry, 1866–1963*. Jefferson, NC: McFarland, 2016.

Louisville Courier-Journal. "Alleged Slayer Sued by Lawyer." June 6, 1928, III, 5.

———. "Bond Denied in Grave Slaying." May 27, 1928, II, 3.

———. "Chair Is Tested." June 11, 1930, 1+.

———. "Death Sentence Given Ratcliffe." December 8, 1928, 1+.

———. "Execution Date for 5 Men Set." May 6, 1930, 1+.

———. "Jury in Ratcliffe Trial Is Discharged." June 28, 1928, 1.

———. "Man Attacked at Grave Dies." May 24, 1928, 24.

———. "Man Slugged, Robbed…." May 21, 1928, 1+.

———. "Murder Case Here Submitted to Jury." June 27, 1928, 1.

———. "Prisoner's Money Attached." May 29, 1928, 26.

———. "Ratcliffe Goes on Trial Again." December 7, 1928, 1+.

———. "Ratcliffe Goes to Trial for Life." June 26, 1928, 1.

———. "Ratcliffe Held Slayer of Muse." June 2, 1928, 22.

———. "Ratcliffe Indicted in Grave Slaying." May 30, 1928, 24.

———. "Ratcliffe to Die in Chair Feb. 11." December 22, 1928, 20.

———. "Ratcliffe Trial Is Delayed Again." December 5, 1928, 24.

———. "Sampson Calls 3 to Hotel." June 12, 1930, 1+.

———. "Second Trial of Ratcliffe Passed." November 28, 1928, 28.

———. "$10,000 Bond Set for Man in Attack, Theft." May 22, 1928, 1.

———. "Two Executed at Eddyville." June 13, 1930, 1+.

BLUE GOON OF KENTUCKY

Louisville Courier-Journal. "'Blue Man' Again Is Proof Against Bullets." January 21, 1921, 2.

———. "'Blue Man' Again Seen…." January 19, 1921, 2.

———. "'Blue Man'—Clever Daring Intruder Here…." January 18, 1921, 2.

———. "'Blue Man' Hunt Uncovers Thefts." January 20, 1921, 1.

———. "'Blue Man' Is Busy Ringing Doorbells." January 29, 1921, 2.

———. "'Blue Man' of Mystery…." January 17, 1921, 1.

———. "'Blue Man' Seen at Eighth and Walnut…." January 24, 1921, 1.

———. "'Blue Man' Vanishes but Leaves Letter." January 22, 1921, 1.

———. "'Blue Woman' Takes Place of 'Blue Man.'" February 2, 1921, 8.

———. "Woman Shoots…." January 23, 1921, I, 1.

BIBLIOGRAPHY

SOME MOTHER'S BOY

Georgetown Times. "Bury Unidentified Young Man in Local Cemetery." April 20, 1921, 1.
————. "Youth Killed by Train, Unidentified." April 6, 1921, 1.
Louisville Courier-Journal. "Unidentified Boy Killed...." April 3, 1921, IV, 7.
WLEX-TV. "Coroner May Have Found Family of 'Some Mother's Boy.'" May 2, 2017.
————. "96 Years Later, 'Some Mother's Boy' Is Going Home." June 13, 2017.
————. "'Some Mother's Boy': Unidentified Body Being Exhumed." March 10, 2017.

PEARL'S HEAD

Louisville Courier-Journal. "Pearl Bryan Tragedy Revived...." November 16, 1900, 7.
————. "Pearl Bryan's Skull Found." February 18, 1907, 1.
————. "Skull of Pearl Bryan Burned in Furnace." March 9, 1907, 2.
McDonald, James, and Joan Christen. *The Perils of Pearl Bryan*. Bloomington, IN: AuthorHouse, 2012.

CIRCUS TROUBLE

Louisville Courier-Journal. "A Circus Bunco Game." November 4, 1914, 4.
————. "The Circus Smash-Up." October 24, 1882, 6.
————. "Cowboys Acquitted." August 12, 1900, I, 4.
————. "Cowboys on Trial." August 11, 1900, 2.
————. "Died of His Injuries." June 7, 1902, 3.
————. "An Easy Victim of Showmen's Wiles...." June 22, 1902, I, 7.
————. "Escapes Lynching." August 3, 1916, 3.
————. "Four Arrested for Wheeler's Death." August 6, 1900, 4.
————. "Girl Kidnapped." June 19, 1902, 7.
————. "In Handcuffs." June 20, 1902, 2.
————. "Kentucky News in Brief." June 23, 1902, 3.
————. "Kentucky News in Brief." September 10, 1902, 4.
————. "Kentucky News in Brief." September 21, 1900, 5.
————. "Lion Tamer Decapitated by Infuriated Beast." April 27, 1915, 7.
————. "P. Is Held to Answer." June 25, 1902, 2.
————. "The Paint Lick Disaster." September 26, 1882, 2.
————. "Paris, Ky." April 25, 1878, 4.
————. "Press Agent Leehy Hit...." June 6, 1902, 8.
————. "Rough Riders of Buckskin Bill's Wild West...." August 5, 1900, I, 7.
————. "Three Men Killed." September 25, 1882, 8.

Owensboro (KY) Messenger and Examiner. "Gone On a Circus." August 22, 1889, 3.

Peter. "A Little Known Wild West Show: Buckskin Bill's." Western Trips, January 21, 2014. https://westerntrips.blogspot.com/2014/01/a-little-known-wild-west-show-buckskin.html.

Don't Get Back to Where You Once Belonged, Jo-Jo

Drimmer, Frederick. *Very Special People.* New York: Bell, 1985.

Kentucky Register (Richmond). "Barrett's Circus." May 6, 1887, 3.

———. "Barrett's Circus Coming." April 15, 1887, 3.

———. "'Gath' on Jo-Jo." April 22, 1887, 3.

———. "Jo-Jo, the World's Enigma." April 29, 1887, 2.

Louisville Courier-Journal. "Death Takes Jo-Jo…." February 7, 1904, I, 3.

———. "Jo-Jo, the Dog-Faced." November 12, 1886, 5.

———. "Jo-Jo, the Dog-Faced Boy." November 11, 1886, 2.

———. "Lived to Be 104." March 21, 1895, 2.

———. "Over Six Feet Tall; Weighed 50 Pounds." November 1, 1906, 3.

Clay County Creepiness

TB Sheets

Walters, Tom, and Laura Johnson. *Clay County, KY, Cemetery Records.* Vol. 2. N.p., 1990.

Hamp Takes Flight

Walters, Tom, and Laura Johnson. *Clay County, KY, Cemetery Records.* Vol. 2. N.p., 1990.

A Self-Made Widow

Louisville Courier-Journal. "Bones Are Found in Ax Slaying Case." April 10, 1931, 7.

———. "Clay Man Gets Death in Slaying." May 5, 1931, 2.

———. "Death Plea Planned for Woman, Neighbor." April 30, 1931, 5.

———. "Man, Woman Indicted in State Ax Slaying." April 21, 1931, 26.

———. "Officers Seek Body After Slaying Charge." April 7, 1931, 18.

———. "Sampson Gives Clemency to 339." December 8, 1931, 1+.

———. "Widow Accused in Clay Slaying." April 6, 1931, 1.

———. "Widow Awaits Killing Verdict." May 1, 1931, 13.

BIBLIOGRAPHY

Feud for Thought

Louisville Courier-Journal. "Abolition of Clay County Is Proposed." February 2, 1933, I, 1.
———. "Alleged Killer Is Slain in Clay." June 25, 1935, 1+.
———. "Clay Funeral Halted by Ambush Shooting." June 21, 1935, I, 8.
———. "Factions Aroused by Clay County Killing." June 20, 1935, 16.
———. "The Situation in Clay." Editorial, February 3, 1933, 6.

THE GREAT MADISON COUNTY MONKEY HOAX

Engle, Fred Allen, and Robert N. Grise. *Madison's Heritage.* Richmond, KY: AA Printing Company, 1985.
Harrodsburg Democrat. "A Startling Phenomenon." Reprinted in *Hopkinsville Semi-Weekly South Kentuckian,* February 18, 1887, 2.
Hopkinsville Semi-Weekly South Kentuckian. "Those Monkey Stories." January 6, 1888, 1.
Houston Post. "The Kentucky Farmer Who…." Editorial, February 26, 1887, 2.
———. "Strikes." February 15, 1887, 2.
Kentucky Register [Richmond, KY] "A First-Class Nuisance." February 25, 1887, 3.
———. "That Monkey Business." February 25, 1887, 3.
Louisville Courier-Journal. "The Hemp-Field Monkeys." March 2, 1887, 3.
———. "In and About Kentucky." August 16, 1889, 4.
———. "A Monkey Story." February 17, 1887, 2.
———. "The Seven Large Monkeys…." Editorial, February 18, 1887, 4.
———. "That Monkey Story." February 19, 1887, 6.
Louisville Times. "Anent the Monkey Story…." Editorial, February 18, 1887, 2.
———. "The Madison Monkey Story." March 4, 1887, 1.
———. "Madison's Monkeys." February 17, 1887, 2.
———. "Monkey Must Go." March 2, 1887, 2.
———. "Over-Credulous People…." Editorial, February 19, 1887, 2.
———. "That Monkey-Labor Lie Has Got Over to Ohio…." Editorial, February 22, 1887, 2.
MacDougall, Curtis. *Hoaxes.* New York: Macmillan, 1940.
New York Sun. "Apes as Workers." Editorial, February 21, 1887, 2.
New York Times. "Monkeys to Be Boycotted." February 17, 1887, 1.
———. "Scab Monkeys." Editorial, February 17, 1887, 4.
Pittsburg Evening Leader. "The Modern Munchausen Has Gone…." October 23, 1904, n.p.
Powell, E.P. *Our Heredity from God.* 2nd edition. New York: Appleton, 1888.
———. *Our Heredity from God.* 5th edition. New York: Appleton, 1901.

BIBLIOGRAPHY

CHARIVARI SHAKEDOWNS

Kaltenbacher, W.S. "Hectic Hemp-Breaking...." *Louisville Courier-Journal*, November 29, 1925, III, 9.

Louisville Courier-Journal. "Boy Fatally Injured in Indiana Charivari." June 21, 1915, 10.

———. "Bridegroom Roughly Handled in Indiana." August 24, 1911, 5.

———. "Charivari Ends in Murder." March 24, 1894, 1.

———. "Charivarists Want Sheriff to Give Back Noise Makers." August 8, 1931, 5.

———. "Death at the Charivari." November 22, 1894, 3.

———. "Governor Asked to End Charivari." August 7, 1931, 5.

———. "The Groom Recalls His Manners." Editorial, August 13, 1931, 6.

———. "Kentucky Notes." December 12, 1911, 6.

———. "Killed at a Charivari." May 2, 1887, 1.

———. "Newlyweds Tired of 13-Day Serenade." August 6, 1931, 2.

———. "The Report of Mr. Reuben Parrish...." Editorial, February 12, 1898, 6.

———. "Resented the Charivari." February 21, 1888, 4.

———. "Serenaders Shot." December 8, 1915, 3.

———. "Shot at Serenaders." February 10, 1898, 5.

———. "Shot by the Groom." December 19, 1889, 1.

———. "Suicide Following an Accidental Shooting...." August 21, 1897, 1.

———. "Ten Girl Well-Wishers of Bride Are Shot." February 9, 1915, 1.

———. "Weary of a Charivari." November 29, 1888, 2.

———. "Wounded at Charivari." June 11, 1913, 4.

PROFESSOR TOBIN BAFFLES LOUISVILLE, THEN THE WORLD

Louisville Courier-Journal. "Although the *Courier-Journal*...." Editorial, June 11, 1882, 4.

———. "In Hoc Signo Vinces." May 31, 1882, 8.

———. "An Interesting Puzzle." May 30, 1882, 6.

———. "Prize Puzzle!" Advertisement. June 1, 1882, 1.

———. "Prof. Tobin Dead." August 5, 1883, 7.

———. "That Tobin Puzzle." July 2, 1882, 9.

———. "That Tobin Puzzle." June 4, 1882, 4.

———. "To Dust." August 6, 1883, 8.

———. "The *Washington Critic*...." Editorial, June 6, 1882, 4.

Magicpedia. "Thomas Tobin." October 10, 2012. https://geniimagazine.com/wiki/index.php?title=Thomas_Tobin.